REQUIEM FOR STEAM THE RAILROAD PHOTOGRAPHS OF DAVID PLOWDEN

W. W. NORTON & COMPANY

NEW YORK • LONDON

REQUIEM FOR STEAM

THE RAILROAD PHOTOGRAPHS OF DAVID PLOWDEN

FOR JIM MAIRS

Requiem for Steam: The Railroad Photographs of David Plowden

Copyright © 2010 by David Plowden
All rights reserved
Printed in Italy · First Edition

The text of this book is composed in FF Scala and FF Thesis "The Mix"
    (FontShop International); the headings are set in Univers UltraCondensed

Design and composition by John Bernstein Design, Inc., New York
Manufacturing by Mondadori Printing, Verona, Italy

FRONTISPIECE DETAIL:
Great Northern Railway, "Extra 3377 East," near Atwater, Minnesota, 1956.
Full image on page 61, with extended caption for image 61 on page 190.

Library of Congress Cataloging-in-Publication Data

Plowden, David.
  Requiem for steam : the railroad photographs of David Plowden. — 1st ed.

    p.   cm.
ISBN: 978-0-393-07908-1 (hardcover)

1. Steam locomotives — History. 2. Steam locomotives — Pictorial works. I. Title.

TR603.P56   2010
779'.9625261092 — dc22   2010016651

W. W. Norton & Company, 500 Fifth Avenue, New York NY 10110
www.wwnorton.com

W. W. Norton & Company Ltd., Castle House, 75/76 Wells Street,
London, W1T 3QT

1 2 3 4 5 6 7 8 9 0

ACKNOWLEDGMENTS

It is particularly difficult for me to thank all of the people who have had a part in making possible the photographs for this book. A great many of these images were made fifty or more years ago and in the ensuing years I have unfortunately forgotten the names of so many who helped me —but not all.

My mother rightfully earns first mention for she was my champion from the very beginning. She drove me down to the Putney depot in Vermont one bright summer day in 1943 when I was eleven so I could take a photograph of the steam engine on the 4:20. But at train time when it hove into sight around the curve north of the station I was stricken with "buck fever" and began to shake so badly I handed the camera to Mother and said, "You take it." She did. But a day or two—maybe a week—thereafter, we were back at the depot. This time I grasped her small red, square box Brownie camera firmly in my hands, stood my ground as the 4:20 bore down on me, fired the shutter, and made my first photograph.

The event at Putney wasn't the only time Mother fostered my love of railroads. She trusted me enough to allow me to take my first solo train trip —between Putney and White River Junction, Vermont—when I was eleven. I kept on riding the rails so much that one of her friends—or was it an aunt of mine?—asked her whether I was just wasting my time riding trains. "He's gathering grist for the mill," she replied. She realized how important my love of the railroads was to me and understood that I wasn't just wasting my time. Before I could drive she would take me out to such godforsaken places in the Jersey Meadows as the Erie's Coxton Yards in Seacaucus, New Jersey, where she would sit in the car for hours while I wandered around the engine terminals taking pictures. She took me on many trips, including my first long-distance ride, from New York to Buffalo and back, in 1946: up on the Empire State Express and back on the Lackawanna's Pocono Express. She was unfazed by the latter's 3:50 a.m. departure. So my dear mother, although you are no longer with us, you will always have my everlasting thanks for understanding my love of railroads and for letting me gather grist for my mill. It's why I am a photographer today.

I also owe a huge debt of gratitude to Minor White, who was one of the world's foremost photographers, with whom I studied in Rochester, New York, in the fall of 1959 and early winter of 1960. He said, "Go do your damned engines. Get them out of your system or you'll never do anything else." At the time I thought his words were spoken in anger and frustration. But I realize now how well he understood my love of steam engines. Because of his words I went directly down east to the CPR in March 1960 to photograph steam's eleventh hour in Montreal, rode the Scoot, and made so many of the photographs in this book.

I must not forget to thank O. Winston Link, for whom I worked in 1958 and 1959. It was Link who gave me two valuable pieces of advice. He told me to always carry a portable darkroom whenever I was in the field for any length of time. More important, he said that in order to succeed you have to dedicate yourself without reservation to whatever it is you do; that this is much easier to do if you don't give a damn what the rest of the world thinks.

Although there are many whose names I have forgotten there were many others I shall never forget. They showed me what railroading was like firsthand. One of these men was Bill Hogan, the conductor on the Rutland's Green Mountain Flyer. I was twelve when I first rode with him and twenty-two the last time I saw him. I will always think of him as one of my grandfathers I never knew. And how could I forget Bill Cannon, the engineer on the southbound Flyer between Rutland and Bellows Falls in whose cab I rode countless times from the age of thirteen until the very day before the diesels came. There was Curley Burns—Mr. Burns—the trainman on the Central Vermont. For years it was a family occasion to go down to the Putney depot to meet his train, Number 717, the 6:20. When I was old enough to ride his trains he always invited me into the baggage car where he and I would sit on a trunk by the open door listening to the engine as the countryside rolled by. It became a tradition for me to ride the engine of his train from Brattleboro to Putney. Whenever the family rode his train he would come back and sit with us. When he died in the mid-1950s it was almost like losing a member of the family. Nor can I forget John M. Caffrey, the conductor on the Lehigh Valley's Asa Packer, who befriended me in 1946 and with whom I rode until he retired in 1961. There were also many an engineer and fireman I knew when I worked for the Great Northern in 1955–56 who let me fire their engines and at times even run them. This was strictly against the rules so they shall have to remain anonymous—but surely not forgotten by me.

I owe a most special debt of gratitude to Mr. D. B. Wallace, the Canadian Pacific Railway's manager of public relations in Montreal. I contacted him in June 1959 and again directly after leaving Minor's workshop in February 1960. On both occasions he said come to Montreal where he gave me a "ticket to heaven": permission to ride any engine, visit any terminal, yard, or roundhouse—any CPR property—all the way from Montreal to St. John, New Brunswick. Without Mr. Wallace's help a great many of my photographs of the steam locomotive would never have been made. Another person who deserves special thanks is William Laidlaw, chief dispatcher for the CPR's Brownville Division. He helped me in so many ways in the summer of 1959 and again in March 1960. I called him on Sunday, March 28, asking if I could ride the Scoot on Wednesday instead of Monday and he said, "I'd come tomorrow if I were you." I did and the return trip from Lac-Mégantic on March 29 turned out to be the last day of steam on the Scoot. Another person I remember is my old friend John Sangster, the CPR's roundhouse foreman at McAdam, New Brunswick. You gave me the run of your domain in the summer of 1959 and again in March 1960. Thank you, too, for building me a darkroom in the basement of your roundhouse where I could develop film. I remember how surprised I was when you drove all the way to New York and to McAdam in the same day to be at the opening of one of my shows. I would also like to thank Doug Blue, the fireman on Scoot's engine on March 29, 1960, for making the picture of a train crossing the Shop Pond viaduct possible. Thanks, too, to his engineer on that day, Bud Rolfe, and the engineer Bob Thombs, with whom I made several memorable trips in the engine of the Scoot in the summer of 1959.

There are many more who come to mind as I search my memory and whose efforts on my behalf I appreciated so much. One was the late Freeman Hubbard, editor of the *Railroad Magazine*, who published so much of my work at the beginning of my career and who arranged access for me on many railroad sites. Thanks, too, to David P. Morgan, editor of *Trains* magazine, for publishing my first photograph on page 29 of the December 1954 issue, which was the beginning of a lifelong relationship with Kalmbach Publishing.

There are a few others who when I asked for their help shared their knowledge with me without hesitation. Without their contributions I could not possibly have completed the technical section of this book. When I say

I owe a great debt of gratitude to you it is not the obligatory "I owe . . . etc." that appears in the acknowledgments section of virtually every book. It is the truth. Many thanks then to Greg McDonnell, for sharing his knowledge about the Sydney & Louisburg with me and for saving me from making several terrible mistakes. Frank Barry, photographer of steam engines and noted expert on railroads, thank you for setting me straight on several crucial pieces of information, including the date of the last official run of CNR steam and subsequent excursions. To Scott Lothes, project director of the Center for Railroad Photography and Art, many thanks for help, in particular, for sharing all your knowledge about Chinese steam, especially the dates of construction of their last locomotives. I also want to express my gratitude to Robert S. McGonigal, the editor of *Classic Trains*. First I want to thank you for using my photographs and my story about the Scoot's last run with steam in your special edition of *Classic Trains* marking the fiftieth anniversary of the year the last steam locomotives were used on class I railroads in the United States and Canada. Quite apart from that I want you to know how much I appreciate the amount of time you spent looking up information and answering multifarious questions about a most important and often obscure fact. John Gruber, founder of the Center for Railroad Photography and Art, you are a friend, indeed, and a veritable font of knowledge on all things railroad. I must have driven you half mad with my innumerable telephone calls and e-mails (including those today) regarding the most arcane and obscure facts that I was unable to track down. You have been kind and patient enough to answer all of them. Thank you! Thank you, too, to my dear friend Bill Young, publisher, writer, photographer, and foremost authority on America's short line railroads, the Tunkhannock and Starrucca viaducts, and just about everything else one would want to know about the history of railroads. Our recent telephone conversations about one piece of information or another brought back so many memories of our days chasing steam: the Iron Horse Rambles, the 614 and the 765. What larks those were, and what a help you were with this project.

I am very grateful to George A. Matheson, a former Canadian Pacific Railway employee who shared his knowledge of the last days of steam on the CPR's Atlantic region with Robert McGonigal who passed the information on to me. It verified when the last runs of the 5107, the 2663, and the 3514 occurred. According to him, the 5107 pulled train Number 517, the Scoot, from Brownville Junction to Lac-Mégantic once again on April 8. On April 9 it pulled the Mégantic-Sherbrooke way-freight and left Sherbrooke for St. Luc Yard in Montreal that evening with freight Number 913. The 5107 was the last live steamer in revenue service out of Sherbrooke. The 2663 made her last run on April 2 from Mégantic to Sherbrooke. The 3514 remained in Mégantic as stationary boiler until early fall before she was towed dead to Montreal to be scrapped in November 1960.

There are others I would like to give a most special word of thanks. Josh Law, my assistant during the past three years, came on board as I was working on *Vanishing Point*. You were a real trouper in the darkroom and made it possible for me to concentrate all of my attention on printing, developing, and toning. When we moved upstairs to the computer you taught me a great deal about PhotoShop. I shall always be grateful to you for your efforts. Morgan Anderson, my former student, now a photographer in his own right and grand master of PhotoShop and my tutor today, is teaching me how to utilize my years of experience as a printmaker in the darkroom to make ink jet prints with the computer. No small task! You helped me make—in some cases you made—all the scans for this book. You always asked me to make the final decision about how anything should look, but often you had to show me the way to achieve the result. I owe you a great debt of gratitude for your patience and for sharing your skills with me. I have enjoyed our collaboration very much. I would also like to say a heartfelt word of thanks to Renée Lalonde. You have helped me organize my work and clean up the mess that constantly threatens to overwhelm my office and me. In a few hours you manage to put everything back to rights. I don't know how you do it but I am glad you do.

A special word of thanks to Bill Rusin who has always been in my corner and has been my champion. Thanks for your faith in my work.

Once again I want to thank John Bernstein for designing another book of mine with such care and respect for my sensibilities. I know I'm not the easiest person to satisfy. However, *Requiem for Steam* is beautiful and I could not be more pleased. Austin O'Driscoll, editorial assistant at W. W. Norton, most certainly did her part in keeping track of all the minute details that might have been overlooked had it not been for her "eagle eye." Thanks for keeping the train on the track.

Of course this book wouldn't exist at all without my editor Jim Mairs. This is the ninth book we have done together during the past thirty years and I never cease to wonder how you always manage to create one out of the mass of photographs I bring you. It is especially true with *Requiem for Steam*. In the beginning there were 183 photographs spread out over the table. Frankly I had no idea how to organize them. You did. When you had finished arranging them we had a book. Sandra watched and said she had never seen anything like the way you worked. I agree, except that I have seen you work your magic many times before. You are rather like the conductor who makes a hundred musicians sound as if the orchestra were a single instrument.

Lastly, I would like to thank my dear wife, Sandra. You have always said you have an "engine block" when it comes to locomotives and steam machines. Because of this impediment you insisted that you contributed nothing whatsoever to this project. Nonsense. You edited the text; you spent hours, days working and reworking the sequence of the photographs. You told me to use only my best photographs, to throw away the "antelope" and keep only the "lions and tigers." You listened to me even when I knew I was driving you to distraction, talking on and on and on about this engine or that, never speaking about anything else except railroads, railroads, railroads! Yet you were always there when I needed encouragement. You stood by me, spurred me on, and forgave me even when I was late for dinner. When I began to doubt whether I could keep up the pace—I worked every day, including weekends, from early July until mid-November—you kept reminding me that this was going to be a beautiful book. You had faith in me as we always have had in each other. We make a wonderful team! Despite your engine block you have always loved the man who loves his engines. I love you back.

CANADIAN PACIFIC RAILWAY LOCOMOTIVE NUMBER 5107. MÉGANTIC, QUEBEC. MARCH 29, 1960.

REQUIEM FOR STEAM

I never understood why Minor White, one of the most influential photographers of the twentieth century, accepted me as a student in one of his workshops. The portfolio I presented to him consisted of twenty badly printed pictures of steam engines. He looked at them once slowly without saying a word, then for a second time even more slowly. After he had finished he remained silent for what seemed an eternity before turning and saying, "You have the eye of a poet."

So began six of the most difficult—and valuable—months of my life. Minor was an exacting taskmaster, a perfectionist. He encouraged us to gain complete mastery of technique by using the Zone System, a method that was developed by Ansel Adams that gave the photographer precise control over his material. He drilled us relentlessly so that we would learn our technique well enough to put it in our back pockets in case we should ever need it. Once there, he said, we could concentrate on the business of making photographs.

He was unquestionably one of the greatest printers who ever lived. He said he couldn't teach us how to print but to come and stand next to him in the darkroom, watch his technique. I did and it proved to be a priceless experience. One of the most important things I remember was Minor's definition of a photographer as being someone who "must have his feet on the ground and his head in the clouds." Abstract art "separates the sheep from the goats" was one of Minor's favorite aphorisms, one he never let us forget. Frankly I was never sure who were the sheep and who were the goats, but I knew that whichever they were I was the other.

Minor's approach to photography and mine proved to be antithetical and soon I found that the pallid aestheticism of the workshop began to stifle me. I yearned for the smell of coal smoke, of hot, dripping grease, of steam and the sweat of the roundhouse and so I decided to leave one night in the middle of a blizzard. My cohorts implored me to stay, saying that I was on the threshold of an epiphany.

Minor wrung his hands despairingly, saying that he had taught me nothing. I assured him he had, which was the truth. He said in parting that all my photographs reflected a feeling of loss. The loss of the steam engine, he surmised. He was right. "Go do your damned engines," he said in frustration "Get them out of your system or you'll never do anything else."

To this day, long after steam locomotives have vanished, they are still very much in my system. From the time I can remember the railroad has been my leitmotif, the recurring theme that appears in one guise or another in so much of my work. Ever since I was a little boy I have spent as much time riding trains as possible. I sought out as many different railroads and trains as I could find, never taking the same route twice if there was an alternative. After a lifetime of riding the rails I have traveled many hundreds of thousands of miles across the length and breadth of the North American continent, from Newfoundland to the Pacific. During all those journeys the railroad became my tutor and the train window was the lens through which I formed my perception of America. No matter where I was going somehow I always found my way to the tracks and so long as there was a train going my way I was on it.

What a wondrous thing this steam engine was. I confess I would never have picked up the camera had it not been for the locomotive. The very first picture I ever made was of a steam engine taken with my mother's little red box Brownie. I was eleven. For fifteen years thereafter I used the camera solely to photograph locomotives and trains. Even when I bought my first "serious" camera, a Crown Graphic, in 1952 I used it only to photograph trains.

I have never been able to fully explain why the locomotive was so compelling to me. Perhaps it is as simple as the fact that the formative period of my life coincided with the twilight of steam and like many a boy I was overcome by the spell of the locomotive. Wherever it appeared it commanded full attention. It was dangerous, magnificent, terrifying, exciting, loud, immense, and powerful all once. No one could tell me that this wasn't the most compelling machine ever devised!

There was nothing covert about a steam engine, nothing hidden from the eye. When at rest it was possible for anyone standing beside it to marvel at this most extraordinary of mechanisms. The system of rods and cranks, valve gears and pistons organized with sublime precision and logic, which took steam and turned it into motion, was laid out as plainly as a blueprint for all to see. In that way it was like a bridge—one does not have to be a structural engineer to understand the accomplishment. Moreover, this example of man's ingeniousness was available for all to behold at the foot of Main Street, at train time at the depot, or steaming across almost any landscape in the world. It was this accessibility, I believe, that was one of the main reasons why the locomotive has had such a powerful grip on our collective imaginations. No other machine could make such a claim.

As I drove east along the thruway on my way home to New York City I kept hearing Minor's words ringing in my ears: "Go do your damned engines. Get them out of your system or you'll never do anything else." He knew I had to photograph them. You're damned right I'm going to photograph my damned engines!

My first attempt at making serious photographs had been when I went "down east" to the Canadian Pacific in the summer of 1959. And now six months later as I headed back east my thoughts were on one thing—where to find enough engines to finish what I had started the previous summer before it was too late. And it was 11:59 for the steam engine in North America.

As I made my way along the snowy thruway I began to think about all the railroads that once had stables full of steam locomotives just a few years ago and how quickly they had disappeared from North America. From the moment the diesel appeared on the scene nearly a generation previously the steam locomotive was biologically extinct in North America. The figures supplied by the Association of American Railroads illustrate this most graphically. In 1925 there was exactly one diesel on the rosters of class 1 railroads in the United States versus 63,614 steam locomotives. By 1950, the year after the last commercially built steam locomotives in the United States were delivered, there were 25,640. Five years later there were 5,982 and 24,746 diesels. Only the Norfolk & Western soldiered on. It continued to build locomotives in its own Roanoke shops from 1950 until 1953. Not surprisingly it built the very last locomotive for service on a North American railroad. Number 244, an 0-8-0 switcher, was delivered in December 1953. By 1960 the diesel had won the day. The steam locomotive had virtually disappeared from every class 1 railroad in the United States. There were just 261 versus 28,278 diesels.

Why had it happened so quickly?

As spellbinding as that most awesome of mechanisms was to behold, from a mechanical point of view the reciprocating steam locomotive was a fundamentally inefficient, uneconomical form of motive power. The very process that utilized the power of expanding steam and converted reciprocating motion into rotary motion—by way of a connecting system of rods and cranks—was extremely difficult to balance, created enormous torque, and was hell on the tracks. The loss of energy was tremendous even in the most well designed locomotive.

It had an insatiable appetite, too, devouring coal by the ton by the mile and drinking thousands of gallons water every hour, both of which had to be replenished frequently on the road. As a result the American landscape in the day of the locomotive was rife with coal docks and water plugs. "Tank towns" and "jerkwater towns" sprouted up beside the tracks where the locomotives stopped to slake their thirst. In addition the locomotive required a whole spectrum of specialized facilities to maintain and service it: back shops, roundhouses, turntables, and ash pits as well as a host of attendants to minister to its demands. The continually rising costs of labor and coal in postwar America was one of the principal reasons for its demise. Only in China, where manpower and coal are cheap and plentiful, did the locomotive survive in large numbers. They were used on the Jitong railway in Inner Mongolia until December 2005, nearly a half century longer than in North America.

Moreover, unlike diesel engines, which were bought off the floor like automobiles, every steam engine was essentially a one-off creation designed to perform a specific task. I knew that no steam engine was like another. On the other hand the diesel was a chameleon. It was infinitely flexible. If more power was needed separate units could be strung together. The same engine could be used on the road, in the yard, and with a few modifications in either freight or passenger service. Like the automobile it was mass-produced.

There were other reasons as well that made the railroads eager to embrace the diesel. Many a railroad's fleet of aging steam engines had been worn out by World War II's unprecedented traffic and sorely needed to be replaced. Then came the economic slowdown of 1953 followed by one in the summer of 1957, which lasted until the following spring. Both caused a sharp decline in the railroad's carloadings. With fewer trains to haul there was less need for motive power. This gave the railroads the opportunity to retire many more steam engines. The coup de grâce was the nationwide steelworkers' strike, which began on July 15, 1959, and lasted for nearly four months. The strike was devastating to the American steel industry—which never fully recovered—and to the steam engine. Existing diesels and those on order were easily able to handle the railroads' greatly diminished traffic. The situation may have been a shade less bleak in Canada where the railroads had taken a more cautious attitude before finally embracing the diesel wholeheartedly. But by the time I drove away from Minor's workshop the diesel had decidedly won the day in Canada as well.

Like all well-informed aficionados of railroading I knew the whereabouts of virtually every working steam locomotive in the United States and Canada in February 1960—and there were damn few. It was inconceivable that they were gone from the Pennsylvania, the Chesapeake & Ohio, the Northern Pacific, the Union Pacific, and the Baltimore & Ohio. Those grand O-8-class Mikados in whose cabs I had ridden and photographed so often while I worked for the Great Northern had been retired along with all the rest of its steam locomotives in 1957. So quickly had the railroads embraced the diesel that many steam engines in their prime, some not even seven years old, had been consigned to the scrap heap. I thought of the Louisville & Nashville's "Big Emmas" and the Nickel Plate's incomparable fleet of Berkshires that had been able to keep the diesels at bay for what seemed forever and were now gone. It was incomprehensible to me that steam whistles no longer echoed up and down the Connecticut River valley as they had ever since I first heard them as a little boy from our hillside farm in Putney, Vermont. The 707, the last of the Central Vermont's ten magnificent T-3- class 2-10-4s, the largest engines in New England, which I admired so much, had been scrapped. Luckily I had caught up with the 707 in White River Junction on its last southbound trip at the end of March 1957. Even the old Rutland Railroad, my best friend while I was growing up, was not impervious to change. The diesels arrived in 1951 and within a year all the beautiful locomotives I had cherished were gone. So what was left?

The Norfolk & Western. It was the last bastion of steam. Despite the fact that virtually every other major American railroad was well along the road to dieselization by the early 1950s, the Norfolk & Western was still building steam locomotives and from all appearances it seemed as though it would continue to do so forever. In fact in 1955, the year I graduated from Yale, there still wasn't a diesel on its property. Its magnificent trio of

classes, the A, the J, and the Y-6b locomotives, which had seemed invincible for so long, were not able to endure. The flood tide of dieselization finally overwhelmed them as it would all steam locomotives. Now, five years later, as I drove along the thruway, only a few bedraggled individuals were living on borrowed time working mine runs out of Williamson, West Virginia. I had no intention of going to the Norfolk & Western anyway. I had worked for O. Winston Link, who considered the Norfolk & Western his private domain, and I wasn't about to poach on his turf. Link, a most accomplished commercial photographer who had graduated from Brooklyn Polytechnic with a degree in civil engineering, was an unqualified master of lighting. In my eyes no one has ever produced photographs of railroading at night as he did.

Okay, forget the N&W! What about the Grand Trunk Western? The Grand Trunk still used a minor flotilla of steam engines. Most notable were its immaculately maintained 4-8-4s assigned to the Detroit-Pontiac-Durand commuter runs, the last regularly scheduled standard-gauge steam-powered passenger trains in the United States. The Grand Trunk was very tempting, but I realized that every rail fan and his brother would have descended on the Grand Trunk and staked a claim beside its tracks. I imagined that trying to compete with them would be like trying to find a place to stand on the banks of the Musconetcong in New Jersey on the opening day of trout season. I wanted no part of that scenario!

So the Grand Trunk was out too. But what about its parent, the Canadian National? I began to reminisce about myriad adventures I'd had chasing down its steam engines. How could I forget the grand adventure of crossing the wilderness of Quebec on a freight train? I remembered, too, the trip John Rogers, my roommate at Yale, and I had made in September 1954. We staked claim to a location somewhere in Ontario next to the CNR's and the CPR's racetracks between Montreal and Toronto. It was all steam day and night; there was nary a diesel in sight. But alas not for long. I knew that the last steam run along that stretch of track was in April of 1959. The few remaining Canadian National steam engines were way out of my reach, confined to the lines around Winnipeg, where the last scheduled run was made from the Pas, Manitoba, to Winnipeg on April 25, 1960.

I bade my own farewell to CNR locomotives at Hamilton, Ontario, in May 1959. Though its huge roundhouse was filled with dead engines, there were a few switchers working the yards and a handful of faithful old Mikados assigned to several local freights. One morning the foreman, Bill Green, invited me to take a walk through the roundhouse with him. He took his time, stopping every so often to look up at the faces of engines waiting to be scrapped. He seemed to remember them all, as if he were walking amongst the gravestones of old friends. Here and there he stopped to talk about one particular engine or another. To him each had its own personality and he knew each one's quirks, those that were staunch and those that weren't. At one point we paused for a long time looking at a still brightly polished little Pacific. I mentioned how beautiful she looked. He turned to me and said, "Let's fire her up. Run her out on the turntable so you can photograph her."

He went off directly to find a hostler. "Make sure there's enough water in her boiler," he said to him. "Then fire her up. Get just enough steam so we can run her onto the turntable and back." It took the better part of two hours to raise steam on the engine. Meanwhile the foreman and I continued our walk so he could say good-bye to his friends.

As soon as there was enough steam to move the Pacific we both climbed into the cab and he backed it out onto the turntable. I took several photographs, then he insisted we go up to the top of the roundhouse roof where I could take some more. After he was sure that I had the photographs I wanted we climbed back down from the roof and up into the Pacific's cab again. Slowly and gently he put her back into her stall, no doubt for the last time. Sadly the pictures didn't amount to much, but I will never forget the occasion. Several months after my visit I received a big wooden box from him. When I opened it inside was the plate from Number 3423, one of the Mikados I had photographed.

If the Canadian National, the Norfolk & Western, and the Grand Trunks were out of the running, what was left? The Duluth, Missabe & Iron Range, one of the last roads to order diesels. I would have given my eyeteeth to photograph one of its 2-8-8-4s, the largest active steam locomotives in the world. I had heard rumors they were still being used occasionally to haul 140-car ore trains down from Minnesota's iron ranges to the docks at Duluth and Two Harbors. I knew firsthand what a spectacle they could make. One weekend I went trout fishing with a friend near the DM&IR's Two Harbors main. Every few hours the silence would be shattered by the sound of one of those mammoth engines battling upgrade through the woods. That was in May 1956. Now, four years later, not only were those same engines a thousand miles away but the steel strike had affected the iron ore–carrying DM&IR more than most lines. How could I be certain whether any of those behemoths would still be working when I arrived? Alas I couldn't.

Well, there was the Illinois Central, one of steam's staunchest friends. It still had a huge stable of locomotives on standby at Paducah, Kentucky, and Carbondale, Illinois. I understood they were used only sporadically and it was too long a drive to make on the off chance I might catch one or two.

Were there any others? I racked my brain. Yes. The narrow-gauge line of the Denver & Rio Grande Western from Durango to Alamosa, Colorado, was still 100 percent steam. But this was hardly the time of year to trek all the way to Colorado. Besides, often there was only one train a week on the line, sometimes only one or two a month, and in winter usually none at all.

There were two other places in Colorado that were still using steam engines. The Colorado & Southern used a lone 2-8-0, Number 641, on its Leadville Branch and the Great Western Railway used them to haul trains during the autumn sugar beet harvest. But February was not harvest time. A few short lines continued to eschew the diesel. Among those I knew were the Buffalo Creek & Gauley, the Virginia Blue Ridge, the Bonhomie, Hattiesburg & Southern, the Mississippian, the Reader, and the Duluth & Northeastern. The most enticing of these lines was the Lake Superior & Ishpeming in Michigan's Upper Peninsula on the shores of Gitche Gumee. I had heard it said through the grapevine that eleven of its 2-8-0s were still being used.

Where else? The Canadian Pacific. Of course!

I had photographed the Canadian Pacific's Atlantic Region the previous summer. It was one of the very last places in America where scores of steam engines were still being used—more even than on the Grand Trunk. They were still in service all the way down east from Montreal to the Bay of Fundy. I knew the line like the palm of my hand. It would be like going home.

My love affair with the steam engine began in northern New England where I first remember hearing a locomotive whistle, most especially the Central Vermont's high-pitched whistles piercing the night as one of its freight trains came down from the north. Those whistles sounded very much like the Canadian Pacific's. I have often looked north for adventure and now once again the north beckoned. My father was British and there is much English blood coursing through my veins, so I have always felt at home in Canada. Wasn't it perfectly logical then that I should turn once again to Canada and the CPR at steam's eleventh hour? What more appropriate place then to hear the last whistle? Plowden, you want to photograph locomotives, then go back to the CPR! Finish what you started last summer.

So to the Canadian Pacific I was bound. Except for the lines around Montreal, the CPR's Atlantic Region in Quebec and across the wilderness of Maine was far away from the madding crowd. There I could commiserate privately with my beloved locomotives and do my best to come to terms with the reality that come spring they would be gone.

My relationship with the Canadian Pacific as a photographer had begun the previous summer when I wrote to the railroad's director of public relations, D. B. Wallace. I remember being surprisingly bold in my letter. I told him that it was imperative to document the steam locomotive before it was gone; that this was the eleventh hour and there was no time to lose. I also said that I intended to make a book from the photographs I would take, which was true. However, it would be six years before it was published, long after the steam locomotive was gone. I ended the letter with what I hoped was a clincher, saying something to the effect that this was the end of an era; that the steam engine was the machine that had transformed the world. To my surprise, in a few days I received an answer from Mr. Wallace inviting me to come to the general offices in Montreal to talk about my proposition.

Within a week I was sitting on the other side of his desk giving a detailed explanation of my intentions. By the end of the meeting I had signed a release form absolving the company of any liability, lest I be ground to pieces beneath one of its locomotive's driving wheels. In return I received a letter giving me permission to ride any locomotive, caboose, freight, or passenger train; to photograph in all CPR's engine terminals. Anywhere. The letter also instructed all CPR employees to assist me in every way possible. As if this ticket to heaven weren't enough, he also provided me with a list of people I could contact in all the crucial places. In short I had been given the run of the Canadian Pacific all the way from Montreal to the Bay of Fundy.

I wasted not a minute. I drove east from Montreal and headed for Maine and New Brunswick, where I spent most of July and August photographing and riding steam engines to my heart's content. I even made an expedition far down east to Nova Scotia's Cape Breton Island to photograph the Sydney & Louisburg Railway, a line that had become a sort of old folks home for U.S. steam locomotives. At the time it had never seen anything resembling a diesel on its property.

And now in the dead of winter I had decided to go back to the CPR. The drive from Minor's was interminable and I wasted not a moment after I arrived home in New York. I gathered up my cameras, bought a case of film, cobbled together a portable darkroom, and called Mr. Wallace once again. He said come straight to Montreal where he gave the same "ticket to heaven" as he had the previous summer—and most important a schedule of when and where the diesels were to arrive.

Thus at the beginning of March 1960 I set out for Montreal behind the wheel of my 1957 Chevrolet, the ex–police car with a row of bullet holes along the left rear fender and a set of springs that had been made for me by a wagon maker on Cape Breton the previous summer. At that moment I had little idea that I had taken the first step of what was to become a lifelong mission of recording our vanishing history. As far as I was concerned I was a most happy Philistine setting forth to photograph my "damned steam engines."

That the three dozen or so locomotives still in service on the CPR's Atlantic Region were 2-8-2s, 2-8-0s, 4-6-0s, 4-6-4s, G-2 or class G3g 4-6-2s was frankly of little interest to me. True, I may have been a connoisseur of locomotives. I knew every fine point of any given engine's appearance and pedigree and can still tell one locomotive from another at a glance in the pages of any book or magazine. But to me a locomotive is a locomotive. Generically all are essentially the same, and it was this generic sense of "locomotiveness" that I was determined to preserve on film for posterity.

For two weeks Montreal was a glorious last hurrah for steam. I took a room in a dismal motel near the CPR's Glen Engine Terminal and set up my darkroom in the bathroom. I chased down every active locomotive in Montreal and its environs and photographed them ceaselessly from first light until dark. I caught them on passenger trains and on freights, on the Hochelaga turn, at Vaudreuil and Rigaud, at ten below zero and in the warmth of the roundhouse. At Windsor Station I made friends with an engineer who invited me to ride with him several times on the run to Rigaud. His train may have been just a lowly commuter run but his engine was one of the Royal Hudsons, once the pride and joy of the CPR's fleet of passenger locomotives. They were called royal because one of them, the 2850, was assigned to the train that had carried King George VI and Queen Mary on their trip across Canada in 1939. Following the journey the Canadian Pacific was granted permission from the royal family to designate the entire class of streamlined Hudson locomotives "Royal" and for them to wear the royal family crown on their running boards. They have been "Royal Hudsons" ever since, the only locomotives outside of Great Britain to be permitted the designation. Ironically the last night I rode with my friend out of Windsor Station the engine was the 2820, the first of the Royals. For all I know it may have been its final run but it was one hell of a ride. We raced down the mainline at eighty miles an hour. Down to the very end those never-say-die Hudsons gave the diesels a run for their money.

Then one morning they began to arrive in earnest. The diesels, all gaudily painted and shining, came with the swiftness of the plague. Suddenly I found myself on hand for one last run after another. I photographed more feverishly than ever, racing against time that was running out. I was at the Glen and St. Luc as one locomotive after another was retired: the 2412, 1262, 5145, 2461, 2408, 2822, 2820, 2426. All friends, all doomed.

Before I left Montreal I made a pilgrimage to the Canadian Pacific's immense Angus Shops where so many of its locomotives had been built and maintained. I got out of my car and started to walk through the snow toward row upon row, literally hundreds of condemned locomotives, some almost brand-new, still resplendent in fresh paint, waiting on what had become death row. Snow had drifted around them often deep enough to bury their driving wheels, which made it seem as if they had been caught in a blizzard and had been frozen in place. Some stood facing each other, their headlights covered with tattered canvas shrouds. Others were coupled together like a line of elephants standing trunk to tail. As I trudged through the snow among them I became aware of an unnatural, eerie silence. All the essence of locomotiveness was gone. There was no fire, no searing heat, no hissing steam, nor smell of hot grease and coal smoke,

only congealed grease and cold steel and dead silence. Suddenly I had the strange feeling that I was walking through a sepulchral sculpture garden amid rows of statuary of mute heroes from antiquity.

I turned and walked away to where I saw signs of life—life and death. Close by the shop buildings themselves I came face to face with a horrible irony. Men, whose faces were covered with masks, were at work with acetylene torches cutting to pieces the hapless locomotives at the head of the line. As I watched I was overcome by the steely indifference exhibited by the very men who had built and cared for these same locomotives and who were now systematically disemboweling them. These engines were my friends; the single most important things in my life were now being desecrated before my eyes. Despite my feelings of horror, I could not help but admire the professionalism of the executioners. Perhaps as a way of masking my grief I drew upon my own nascent professionalism. I set up my cameras and went to work recording the death of the locomotive in the most graphic terms. Many years later I was reminded of this scene when I was photographing the killing floor of an abattoir in Chicago. Although the dismembering of locomotives is hardly on the same scale as the slaughtering of cattle, to me they were analogous. On the killing floor the men went about their awful task with the same cool indifference I saw at the Angus Shops.

Despite the distance the camera places between you and what you are photographing, the scene soon became too much for me to endure. I turned and walked back to my car through a snowfield strewn with rusted parts of eviscerated locomotives. I drove away greatly disturbed, realizing it was only a matter of a few weeks now before time would run out on the last, few survivors. My experience at Angus galvanized my determination to photograph all the things I cherished and which I realized were going to disappear. It was to become a way of life.

It was time to leave. The diesels were already taking Montreal by storm. There was barely time to stay one step ahead of the diesels down east. I paid a last visit to Mr. Wallace to thank him. He provided me with an updated list of where and when the diesels would arrive. I realized I had barely a week or two at best to complete my mission.

I hastened east to the Quebec Central. When I arrived in Vallée-Jonction, I presented my credentials to the roundhouse foreman and stayed three days. I had beaten the diesels! The CPR's subsidiary the "Quebec Central" was the domain of some of the most impeccably maintained engines I'd ever seen. The stable consisted of old Ten Wheelers and Pacifics dating from before World War I, several of which had Quebec Central lettered on their tenders. There was also a lone CPR class G-5 Pacific, Number 1217, one of the very last Pacific types ever built.

I chased trains up and down the valley of the Chaudière River, past Ste. Marie and on to Scott Jonction through one of the most unspoiled, bucolic landscapes imaginable. It seemed ironic that these coal-fired steam engines never seemed to intrude on this pristine snow-covered farmland. Maybe this was so because to me steam engines were never intrusive wherever they were. This was especially true during my visit to the Quebec Central in early March 1960 when there were so few trains to disturb the peace. The right-of-way was barely visible, hardly a scar on the face of the land. In many places snow had drifted over the tracks and lay hidden until a train passed by and dusted them off.

As magical as my sojourn in Vallée-Jonction had been, I was disappointed from a photographic point of view. I came away with only three "keepers." Three photographs in two days! An excellent catch by my standards today, but in 1960 I was desperate to photograph every last steam engine I could track down. I was also just starting my career and I expected a masterpiece to emerge every time I fired the shutter. What nonsense. I hadn't the experience to realize that photographing isn't vacuum cleaning. I also made the mistake of believing that because I was so happy on the Quebec Central I should have come away with a whole creel full of photographs that mirrored my feelings. Perhaps I didn't realize that what moved me so much about the Quebec Central wasn't photographable. This is so often the case, as I have discovered after more than fifty years behind the camera. I learned a priceless lesson about the limitations of photography on the Quebec Central, a place where I felt at peace with myself: the inability to express in visual terms so many of our innermost feelings. Minor had often used the term "equivalent." I had yet to comprehend the concept of metaphor.

Vallée-Jonction may have been Shangri-la way down east. Yet I felt I had bigger fish to fry on the main line and headed straight for my old haunts in New Brunswick, where I had spent much time the previous summer. It was a long way on snowy roads. By the time I arrived time had almost run out.

McAdam, New Brunswick, was once a bustling, smoky old railroad town way down east, like White River Junction, in the verdant fields of Vermont, where one would never expect to find such a place. By rights it should have been tucked away in some West Virginia or Pennsylvania valley, where railroads and coal smoke were part of the scheme of things.

Mr. Wallace had told me the previous summer that "big power" was still being used on the main line out of there and that there were steam engines in profusion on numerous branch lines radiating out of McAdam into New Brunswick. He was right. When I arrived there in July 1959 McAdam was everything a traditional railroad terminal should have been. It had a locomotive and car repair shop and a huge roundhouse from which a veritable flotilla of locomotives was dispatched each day. It also had a freight yard where a switch engine or two were kept busy shunting cars night and day.

No matter where, the engine terminal was one my favorite haunts. McAdam's was no exception. It was an honest working place, all business, a grimy, hurly-burly, noisy domain of the locomotive, a world of men and machines where the unique relationship between the two was self-evident. As I walked among immense, live locomotives, I could feel the searing heat from their fires, smell the hot grease, and contemplate the wondrous mechanism of the rods and driving wheels that took the power of steam and turned it into motion. I would spend hours in the terminals, mesmerized, watching men performing the rituals of servicing the locomotives and—in the case of the Canadian Pacific—washing every engine. The servicing of these big, burly machines was all "bull work," a world apart from the job requirements of today's high-tech world, which requires another, far more cerebral set of skills. Too often today's mechanic is but an adjunct of the parts department, simply replacing a defective part rather than knowing how to repair it.

In McAdam it was obvious that a mechanic was still a mechanic. Those men I watched at work in the roundhouse took great pride in what they did. If something needed to be repaired a blacksmith or pipe fitter rolled up his sleeves, got out the jacks and chains and welding torches or whatever was needed, and fixed it. Call it skill or pride, or a combination of both, but whatever had to be done these men would find a way to do it. In 1959, when steam locomotives were no longer undergoing classified repairs in the back-shops, the ingenuity of these men was often taxed to the limit.

One such man was John Sangster, the roundhouse foreman on the four to midnight shift, who had befriended me in the summer of 1959. His roundhouse became my house, as did his family's kitchen table where I spent many an evening with John and his family. He became intrigued with the idea that I was genuinely interested in documenting his world and went out of his way to help me get the photographs I needed. One day I mentioned to him that I wished I could find a darkroom in which to develop film. The very next afternoon he took me down to the basement of the roundhouse. He opened the door to a room where he had had his carpenters and pipe fitters build a darkroom for me complete with a sink and hot and cold water. Until the day I die I will never forget John and the little darkroom he had made for me.

When I arrived that dismal day in the winter of 1960 there was hardly any smoke hanging over McAdam. There was no more "big power," no more steam on the "high iron" to the Atlantic. McAdam was on the verge of becoming defunct. The yard was filled with dead, snow-covered engines waiting to be scrapped. I stayed about ten days, long enough to photograph the few live engines that were still under John's care in his grand old roundhouse. My darkroom was still there but there was no time to develop film. No time at all. I photographed feverishly, chasing down every steam engine I could find in New Brunswick—several old ten wheelers and a few G-2 Pacifics still used on branch line turns. Once or twice a switcher was fired up for a shift in the yard when there weren't enough diesels to go around. But that was all.

John's roundhouse was full of lifeless engines as well, standing mutely in their stalls. On most a sign hung from their headlights. *Boiler Empty*, which proclaimed in block capitals "Condemned!" As I walked among them I became overwhelmed by sadness knowing full well that none of them would ever again be vibrant, fire-breathing creatures. I looked upon their faces staring straight ahead out the windows and could not help imbuing them with human emotions. The longer I stayed the more I imagined that they yearned to be free once again. But it was not to be. They were dead. McAdam was dead. And my world was dying.

I had to move on…to one last place. To Brownville Junction, the home of the "Scoot."

The Scoot would probably never have been known to me, or anyone outside of the remote regions of Piscataquis and Somerset counties in Maine, had it not been for the fact that it was one of the very last regularly scheduled trains in the United States to be powered by a steam engine. The only others were the commuter trains operated by the Grand Trunk out of Detroit and the Silverton, which operated as a tourist train in the summer months on the Denver & Rio Grande Western's narrow-gauge line between Durango and Silverton, Colorado.

The Scoot was anything but a tourist attraction. It was a no-nonsense mixed train that ran between Brownville Junction, Maine, and Lac-Mégantic on the other side of the Boundary Mountains in Quebec. It was an institution in that part of Maine, being the only connection with the outside world to those who lived along its route. At 7:15 Eastern Standard Time each Monday, Wednesday, and Friday morning it would leave Brownville Junction and each Tuesday, Thursday, and Saturday it would return from Mégantic at the same time. According to the schedule it was to leave at 7:15; however, it left whenever the train was put together. Once on the road the Scoot would spend the better part of the day meandering through the north woods, setting out and picking up a car of lumber or pulp wood here and there along the way until finally it reached its destination sometime midafternoon, or later, depending on how much switching had to be done along the way. Although the timetable listed fixed departure times at various stations, to say the Scoot kept to any schedule would be stretching a point. It stopped almost anywhere to let off a family of campers or to pick them up at a road or trailhead in the middle of nowhere. I remember being in the cab of the 5137—one of the engines assigned to the Scoot in the summer of 1959—when a fisherman stepped up from the bank of a stream and hailed the engine at some remote spot. Bob Thombs, the engineer, stopped and the fisherman climbed up into the cab and rode the engine a few miles to the next promising stretch of water. Before he climbed down from the cab he gave Bob and the fireman each a nice brook trout from his creel by way of thanks.

Much of that part of Maine, which the Canadian Pacific traverses, was without roads—and, remarkably, still is. When I first rode the Scoot in July 1959 the Canadian Pacific was virtually the only means of transportation in that corner of America. There were only two towns of any size on the Scoot's route: Jackman Station on the U.S. side of the border with Quebec, which combined with the adjacent Jackman proper, had but eight hundred residents; and Greenville Junction, the station for Greenville on Moosehead Lake, boasted a "metropolitan" area with a population of 1,640. The rest of the places on the timetable could not be called communities by any stretch of the imagination. Most were simply passing tracks, or siding graced by a name, the others no more than a collection of houses or cabins around a sawmill or a passing track beside a lake, places with names like Bodfish, Attean, Brassua, Squaw Brook, Camp 12, Morkill, Tarratine, and Holeb. The Scoot could be flagged at twenty-nine places listed in the timetable, aside from its three regular stops at Onawa, Greenville Junction, and Jackman, on its 117-mile trek between Brownville Junction and Mégantic. But, as the fisherman had done, a person could flag it down anywhere along its route.

Greenville Junction was by far the most important station and boasted a small, if elegant, old red frame depot with a semicircular tower at one end. As I remember the waiting room was filled with light, which streamed through the windows on sunny days. Several posters adorned the walls between the windows. No doubt one depicted a Canadian Pacific train in the Rockies and another featured one of its great white steamships, perhaps the *Empress of Scotland* arriving at some port in the Orient. Maybe in fact there were no posters at all, but in my imagination they were there. After all this was a Canadian Pacific station, which by its own admission "Spanned the World."

With or without posters the waiting room at faraway Greenville Junction would have been a wonderful place to anticipate a journey. However, I never saw a solitary soul waiting for "train time." By the time I rode the Scoot the line's only passenger trains, Numbers 41 and 42, stopped at 2:36 and 2:04 a.m., respectively—and only if flagged. And I never saw anyone get on or off the Scoot's coach at Greenville Junction.

Passengers notwithstanding, the Scoot's schedule allotted half an hour to switch cars or for its engine to make a run down the spur into Greenville proper to pick up or drop off a car of lumber or coal. The engine always took water at one of the Canadian Pacific's trademark wooden-sheathed water towers across the tracks at the north end of the platform.

The reason Greenville Junction was a junction was that a branch of the Bangor & Aroostook connected with the CPR. In the 1950s after Brownville Junction became the main interchange between the two railroads the Greenville line was used only as a marginal branch and was finally abandoned altogether. Although the Bangor & Aroostook had been officially dieselized in 1952, the old Bunker Brook Trestle on the Greenville Branch was too feeble to carry the weight of a single diesel engine. Before the problem was finally solved by removing ten tons of weight from the railroad's lightest diesel, the Bangor & Aroostook's last active steam engine pulled the branch's daily—except Sunday—mixed train for several years. I saw it once in July 1949, when engine Number 93, a sporty little ten wheeler, built in 1911, was still in charge.

South of the station was an old "Armstrong" turntable where the Bangor & Aroostook engines used to be turned. By the time I came to Greenville in the summer of 1959 the branch was defunct. However, the B&A's turntable was still there among the weeds and the Queen Anne's lace and was used occasionally by the CPR to turn the engine of a work train.

An Armstrong turntable has no motor; its sole power is manpower. A heavy wooden pole is inserted into a socket at each end of the turntable where the engineer and fireman—or anybody else who wanted to lend a hand—put their shoulders to the poles and started pushing. The turntable groaned and creaked as the engine was laboriously turned. The ancient relic at Greenville was still so well balanced, however, that two men could turn a hundred-and-fifty-ton locomotive with relative ease.

Several times during the summer I spent the night in Greenville so as to be able to photograph the Scoot or a work train in action at one of the few highway crossings between Brownville and Jackman. I stayed in a lovely old white frame guesthouse on a hill on the outskirts of town run by an elderly lady. Memory is a wonderful thing even if not precise. It sifts all the trivia and recalls the essence of what was important. In this case it was the details that made up the character of that room. When I close my eyes I can still remember everything as if I were still there half asleep in the predawn light. The floor creaked when you stepped on it and was covered by several hooked rugs. My room had a huge bed with a comforter on which were two needlepoint pillows. On the walls were hung three lithographs of birds. If memory serves me one was of a catbird on a branch of a blackberry bush, another of a pair of whip-poor-wills, and the third of a barn swallow on its nest. There was a big easy chair in one corner and a washbasin with a hard rubber plug on a chain in the other. On either side of the mirror over the bureau were two photographs taken at the turn of the century: one, on the left, of a man with a neatly trimmed mustache set in a round gilded frame and the other, in a plain wooden rectangular frame, of a woman with her hair done up in a bun. Her mother and father, I surmised? There were immense windows with lace curtains on two sides of the room, which looked out on a beautifully tended flower garden, the kind that one finds only in New England, filled with lupine, iris, and delphinium. I kept the windows open all night and heard whip-poor-wills calling to each other in the distance. In the early morning, before the sun burned off the mist, the room was suffused with the smell of flowers and the songs of myriad birds. One morning I remember being awakened by the sound of the work train's engine whistling in the distance. It reminded me of all the times as a boy in Putney when I used to listen to a Central Vermont train whistle echoing through the hills. That morning in my room outside of Greenville the whistle was even more poignant, a baleful, mournful sound, which grew fainter and fainter as I listened. I lay in bed until the only sounds I could hear were of the birds singing in the garden. I was deeply saddened as I realized it would be one of the last times I'd ever hear a steam whistle.

Greenville Junction was special to me in another way. It's where I met Bob Hardy. Bob was a young boy, maybe ten or eleven, who came down to the depot to meet the Scoot. He reminded me of myself, as a boy, when I used to spend countless hours at the Putney depot watching trains train. As soon as he heard the Scoot whistling east of town Bob would run up to the end of the platform to be next to the engine when it stopped by the water spout. He would watch raptly as the fireman filled the engine's tender with water or walk around beside Bob Thombs, or whoever was the engineer that day, as he oiled 'round the engine. If the Scoot was meeting a train or had to make a run down the spur into town Bob would invariably be invited up into the cab. Whenever there was a work train engine to be turned on the old Armstrong turntable Bob would be there, too, a little mite of a fellow, pushing for all his worth, next to one of the crew members. He and I struck up a friendship of sorts in the course of the summer. I took several photo-graphs of him, including one at the turntable, which I sent him. We kept up a correspondence for several years but our paths diverged and I have often wondered what happened to my little friend at the depot.

The line past Greenville Junction's depot was the very antithesis of the Boston & Maine's Connecticut River line through Putney that I had known so well as a boy. The platform on which Bob Hardy stood waiting for the Scoot was on the Canadian Pacific's "High Iron" to the Atlantic, an integral part of its transcontinental railway system. The line across Maine was established because Canada had much grain to export and when the Great Lakes froze up in the winter it needed a warm water port on the Atlantic coast.

The Canadian Pacific chose a route from Montreal straight across Maine to St. John, New Brunswick, on the Bay of Fundy. After many diffi-culties in construction the line was finally opened in December 1888. For the next seventy years the CPR's line across Maine served as a crucial link in the chain of a most remarkable transportation system that brought prairie wheat from two thousand miles away to the Atlantic—and the rest of the world.

In time this system of exporting grain was to change profoundly. When the new St. Lawrence Seaway opened in 1959 foreign vessels could sail all the way to the Head of the Lakes and back from any port in the world. Thus the CPR's share of grain traffic to the Atlantic dwindled until it became a mere trickle.

Finally in 1988 the Canadian Pacific decided to divest itself of what was now an increasingly unprofitable enterprise. The Canadian Atlantic Railway was formed to take over all operations east of Mégantic. Then in 1994 the CPR sold all its lines east of Montreal to various companies, which attempted to cobble together some semblance of direct rail service along the CPR's erstwhile "high iron" to the Atlantic.

By the end of my visit to the CPR in March 1960 virtually every one of its trains east of Montreal had been desielized. Everything except that venerable institution the Scoot. I called Bill Laidlaw, the chief dispatcher, at Brownville Junction, from McAdam to make sure. "Yes," he said, "it's still steam powered—for now." There was a sense of urgency in those words "for now." It was time to go. I bade farewell to John Sangster, took one last look at McAdam, and headed for Brownville Junction. It was a long way, all blue roads and lots of snow. By the time I reached Milo it was late. I was dog tired from weeks of photographing. I decided that rather than catch the Scoot at 7:15 the next morning, as I had arranged with Bill Laidlaw, I would spend the night in Milo and catch the Scoot's next trip, two days later. I called Mr. Laidlaw at home and asked him if he would mind if I changed my plans.

"Well, David," I heard his voice on the other end of the telephone say, "I'd come tomorrow if I were you."

I packed up and was off within twenty minutes.

I arrived in Brownville Junction long before first light and went straight to the roundhouse foreman, who told me it was good I was here because the diesels were coming "any day now." I went inside the immense circular roundhouse and walked past stalls of silent engines staring straight ahead, like those I'd seen in McAdam. I looked for the 5137, in whose cab I had often ridden last summer. But it was not there. No doubt it had been sent to Angus and might already have been scrapped. In the last stall I came upon the 5107, the engine that had been called for the Scoot that morning, steaming away reassuringly. I took a shower in the locker room and went into town for breakfast.

If ever there was a place that seemed out of step with its time it was Brownville Junction. When I first saw it in July 1959 I felt as if I had stumbled into one of those railroad towns on the edge of civilization that I knew only from the pages of illustrated histories of the old west. Brownville Junction, in fact, was not on the edge of civilization. It was civilization in that part of Maine. All else was forest.

Brownville Junction came into being because the railroad needed to be there. Like all railroad towns its existence depended on the fortunes of the railroad, just as a mining town lived or died in direct proportion to the depth of the vein of coal or ore. It was a junction, but only peripherally. The Canadian Pacific interchanged cars of paper pulp with a branch of the Bangor & Aroostook. Its main role was as an engine terminal and freight yard midway across Maine between McAdam, New Brunswick, and Lac-Mégantic, Quebec.

As I remember it Brownville Junction was a collection of nondescript storefronts clustered along both sides of a stretch of largely unpaved roadway that served as "Main Street." The only place that passed for a hotel was a shabby old building with a bar on the first floor and three rooms on the floor above, which the owner could sometimes be persuaded to rent by the week. I had stayed there the summer before while riding the Scoot. Because I was "known to the company," as he put it, I was let the corner room for seventy-five dollars a week and allowed to use the single shared bathroom as my darkroom at night "so long as no one needed to go"—which happened only once.

After the bar closed the only traffic I saw on Main Street was a young bull moose who came trotting in and out of town every night on schedule as if the Canadian Pacific regulated his life too.

A railroad never sleeps—the yard and engine terminal at Brownville Junction were abustle night and day. All night long came the sound of freight cars crashing together as they were being switched and the incessant huffing and puffing of the yard's switch engine. The morning of March 28, 1960, was no different; the old engine was busily at work putting together the Scoot's assortment of cars.

After breakfast I stopped to see Bill Laidlaw to thank him for telling me to come today. He reiterated the fact that the diesels were on their way. Then he and I walked across the yard toward the roundhouse where the 5107 was already outside with a full head of steam, standing impatiently as the hostler was performing all the servicing rituals to make it ready for its run. He introduced me to the engineer, Bud Rolf, and his fireman, Doug Blue. Then the three of us climbed up into the cab.

The 5107 was a classic old freight "hog." Classic because it was a typical 2-8-2, or Mikado, one of the most widely used locomotive types in the world. In point of fact since it was first introduced in 1887 it was used by all but a handful of the major American railroads. In all more than eleven thousand of them were built. The Canadian Pacific at one time owned a total of 324. Its locomotive Number 5473, completed in 1948, had the distinction of being the last Mikado built for standard-gauge service in North America.

The 5107 was one of twenty class P-1a engines built in 1912 by the same Angus shops in Montreal where I had seen so many of its kind being disemboweled. The engines of the P-1a class, including the 5107, were rebuilt at Angus between 1926 and 1930 and reclassified as P-1ds. Although the "Mike," as the Mikado was affectionately called, was by no means a super power locomotive, its versatility was demonstrated by the fact that the very last steam locomotives ever built were three SY class 2-8-2s assembled from previously existing parts in Tangshan, China, in October 1999.

Winter doesn't give up easily in Maine and March 28 was a beautiful, crystal clear day with the temperature nearly zero. Except for the sense of foreboding I felt the trip to Mégantic was everything an engine ride could be. I sat on the seat box on Doug's side of the cab soaking up all the familiar locomotive sounds I had known since childhood as the old 5107 roared, howling across Maine, up over the Boundary Mountains and down into Lac-Mégantic. The ride was a mélange of exhilarating sensations. The only thing I remember specifically occurred as we crossed the Ship Pond Stream Viaduct. I mentioned to Doug that as a boy I had seen a picture of a train on it in *Railroad Magazine* and always wished I could make one myself.

In Mégantic I took a room in the same hotel across from the station where I had stayed the summer before. After dinner I went to bed, but there was too much on my mind to sleep. Shortly after midnight I dressed, packed up my gear, and went down to the roundhouse, where I spent the rest of the night in the cab of the 5107.

A roundhouse, the engine room of a steam vessel, and an open-hearth shop in a steel mill are three of the most remarkable spaces I have ever known. For those who do not know them I would be hard-pressed to describe what they are like. To say that a roundhouse is reminiscent of a stable is not the cliché it would seem. It was always warm, and I imagined the sounds of locomotives sighing and thumping away in the semidark to be the breathing of leviathan creatures. Whenever there I understood what was meant by "iron horse." The engines that seemed alive and at rest in their stalls were infinitely approachable. It was possible to walk among them and contemplate their wondrous mechanism. In the roundhouse they were not unattended but were under the watchful eye of the hostler, whose very name means "one who takes care of horses." He came by at regular intervals to tend the fires and make sure that there was enough water in their boilers.

Aside from the 5107, there were two other engines under steam with Mégantic that night. One was an ancient 2-8-0, Number 3514, which was to serve as the switcher in the yard, because the regular diesel switcher had been called out on snowplow duty. The 3514, incidentally, was a stationary boiler until November 1960, when it was hauled away dead, to be scrapped.

As such it was probably the last steam engine in the Atlantic Region. The other was Number 2663, a class G-2 Pacific, which was to head west to Sherbrooke in the morning with the local freight.

Dawn on the twenty-ninth found me on top of the coal dock photographing the yard, which was bathed in steam from the three engines that were setting forth to work. After nearly freezing to death I climbed down and went back to the roundhouse to thaw out. Bud and Doug were already there and gave me the news. The diesels were here! One was reputed to be in Brownville Junction being prepared to head the Scoot on its next trip to Mégantic. Two diesels were to arrive in Mégantic on the local from Sherbrooke that very afternoon to take over the duties of the 3514 and the 2663.

I was stunned. This was it, the moment I had dreaded for years. How to cope? By photographing with all your heart, Plowden. I went outside into the freezing cold once again and did my best to record the 5107 while it was being serviced one last time. The roundhouse foreman stopped me and asked if I would take a photograph of himself and his crew with the old 3514. I said, "Of course," and the locomotive was brought up in front of the station. Suddenly what seemed to have been everybody on the Canadian Pacific's payroll in Mégantic that morning came forth to be photographed. They took their places beside the engine and on its running boards and stood still proudly in the freezing cold to be recorded for posterity.

Seeing the men standing beside the 3514 reminded me of those nineteenth-century photographs that were taken to celebrate an occasion: the members of an engine company in front of a firehouse; the captain and his crew posing before the pilothouse of a steamer; a logging crew standing on top of a just felled redwood. There were others depicting a brand-new locomotive, fresh from the erecting shop, posed with all the men who had had anything to do with its construction standing proudly beside it. It was evident from the faces that, whoever they were, they were proud to be there. Remembering those old photographs made the picture I was about to make all the more poignant.

This was not a celebration. The arrival of the diesels meant that many of the men in my picture would be out of a job tomorrow or soon thereafter. They knew the significance of the occasion only too well, as did I. I happened to be the one person with a camera present to capture that portentous moment on film. The photograph I made may have been the record of a little piece of history. It was much more. It was a souvenir, which in the last analysis may be a photograph's most important role, like the pictures taken on vacation to preserve a wonderful time that will soon be over and then carefully put in an album where they will remain as evidence of a long-ago experience until the image itself fades. That long-ago morning in Mégantic was not the last time I was on hand for such an occasion. Since then I have borne witness to far too many.

When I climbed up into the cab of the 5107 I was fully aware of the significance of what was about to happen. Yet strangely nothing seemed any different. Reality was the 5107 now, not the fact that it wouldn't be here tomorrow. The engine, the cab, the sounds, the smells were all familiar and reassuring. As I watched Bud perform the rituals of departure that I had seen a hundred times before, I kept saying to myself, Be aware of what's happening! Drink it all in. This is the last time you will ever ride in the cab of a steam engine again! Ever!

I had my Rolleiflex around my neck ready to go to work. I needed a souvenir. But what to photograph? How could I capture how I felt, convey the significance of this moment? I looked for something tangible that would express my emotions, something that would say to anyone generations hence that this is the way it was on March 29, 1960, in Lac-Mégantic, Quebec. That this was the end of an era. Where was the indisputable evidence proclaiming this was different from all other mornings? I was in despair. Then it dawned on me. Perhaps there was nothing more to say. I had been photographing my heart out for nearly a month. Perhaps now the time had come to put the cameras away and sit quietly in the cab absorbing everything about the steam engine I loved so much.

From my vantage point on the left-hand side of the cab I looked down and saw Bud begin the ritual of "oiling-round." I watched him as I had Brown and Mr. Willard and countless other engineers before. I wondered what was going through his mind as he walked methodically beside the running gear, thrusting his long spouted oilcan here and there to leave a drop or two of precious lubricant on some crucial part. He stopped at the eccentric crank, the linchpin of the running gear, the crosshead bearing where he put the back of his bare hand on each to feel its temperature. There was nothing casual about the way he, or any before him, went about

the task. As I watched I realized this ritual was something he must have performed so many times it had become innate, part of his life as an engineer. I wondered how he would feel on the Scoot's next trip sitting behind the immaculate consul in the diesel's cab? There would be no need for this ritual.

When he had finished the conductor came up with a sheaf of orders in his hand. The two men read them together and compared watches. They said a few words and then Bud climbed up into the cab. He showed the orders to Doug, walked to the right-hand side of the cab, took a wad of cotton waste out of his seat box, and wiped off the throttle and the brake levers. Then he checked the water glass and the boiler pressure gauge and, when he was sure everything was in order, he wiped off his seat box and sat down. In a moment the signal for the brake test filled the cab. A minute or two later the test was made and we were set to go.

I felt strangely detached as if there were an impenetrable block that would not allow me to comprehend the full significance of what was taking place.

Suddenly I was aware of the sound of rushing steam being blown out of the cylinder cocks. I heard the 5107's first deep breath. Our departure was without fanfare of any sort. Except for a wave or two from the group of men by the yard office, there was nothing visibly different from any other morning when the Scoot departed, except perhaps that it was colder than usual. There was no bunting draped over the 5107's pilot beam proclaiming "Last Run of Steam Engine" or something of the sort; no TV cameras or newspaper reporter eager for interviews with the crew about "how they felt." In fact as far as I could tell I was the only person on hand that fateful morning who wasn't an established employee of the railroad.

The sun was well up by now and the light caught the engine's driving rods flashing back and forth as we picked our way through the switches and out of Mégantic. Then all at once I felt a great surge of power as Bud pulled back the throttle and we began the assault up the grade on the west slope of the Boundary Mountains. I turned and looked back at the line of cars following behind us under a cloud of steam and smoke, which rained soot down on the snow-covered foothills and pastures. (I was so engrossed with the 5107 that I had no idea until many years later that the last car of the Scoot that morning was the Fort Simpson, an open-end observation sleeping car, which served as the pay car for CPR employees in Maine—the very last pay car in use on any North American railroad. When it was retired after its last run on July 5 and 6, 1960, another railroad tradition died.) We passed by a few farms before all signs of humanity disappeared as the 5107 and the Scoot plunged into a roadless wilderness. There was nothing but snow and trees and sky, except the smoke. It hung like a contrail in the still air for miles behind us—much like man himself, I thought, whose presence will be felt long after he is gone. Yet, like the smoke, too, all that humanity has achieved will dissipate as surely as that contrail.

For now man and his machine were in full command, as the steady cadence of the engine's exhaust confirmed beyond a doubt. The power of the engine was magnificent. It was as if the 5107 had drawn upon all of its remaining energy to surmount this, its final obstacle. I leaned out of the cab listening to the old engine's relentless assault. As it stormed its way upgrade its thundering voice shattered the silence, drowning out all else, and made goose pimples rise on the back of my neck. Here on that morning in the wilderness those old adversaries technology and nature were once again pitted against each other. The locomotive by its sheer power and unfaltering stride gave the illusion for the moment, at least, that it had cowed all else. But nature, I knew full well, was biding its time.

I looked down from my seat in the cab at the wondrous mechanism: rods and pistons and wheels all orchestrated in unison to drive the engine onward. I looked across the cab at Bud, one of the last men in America to put his hand on the throttle of a steam locomotive. If he was aware of the significance of who he was at that moment his demeanor gave no clue. This taciturn old New Englander in bib overalls and a checkered cap, who looked as much a farmer as engineer, was destined by fate to portray the role of "engineer" ever after in my eyes. He had assumed the same classic pose as all locomotive engineers I remembered—Brown, Bill Cannon, Johnson, "Babe" Mylenbeck, and myriad others in whose cabs I had ridden —hunkered down on the seat box, left hand draped over the throttle, head inclined toward the window so as to be able to hear the exhaust, and, by listening, to better understand his engine and how to make it perform. I looked at Bud and remembered the words of Johnson in whose cab I often rode while working for the Great Northern: "I listen to the exhaust. It tells me everything. Just like playing the piano by ear."

As we neared the summit I was suddenly overcome by a sense of despair. Despite the fact that this was only the beginning of the journey, it might as well already be over. Was this the last time a steam locomotive would storm the mountains, shatter the silence of the forest? Be aware! Don't be beguiled because it is all so familiar. This is not the same experience you have had a hundred times before. This is the last time.

As the 5107 lifted the Scoot over the top and crossed into Maine I imagined I was able to see the expanse of the wilderness laid out before me stretching away forever. Then I saw the locomotive itself in a different light. It was no longer the all powerful machine that had overcome the mountains, but merely a foot soldier in mankind's conquering legions that had achieved only temporary dominion over the earth. The steam hanging in the air and the smoke that drifted away amongst the pine boughs would soon dissipate. The echo of the 5107's exhaust would soon be swallowed by the forest. Silence would reign once again in the north woods. The locomotive, too, was about to be silenced by another machine, a casualty of that inexorable progression by which everything is replaced by something else. Rather like us, I thought, mayflies hatched upon the river of life, to procreate, to flicker, to die only to be borne away by the current.

It was all downhill now. Once again the 5107 seemed to defy its age, fairly freewheeling along the Moose River with all the exuberance of youth. It burst upon Holeb whistle howling, a mournful, spine-tingling cry, as if to raise the ghosts of times past. We raced by leaving once again only a trace of smoke and steam, an echo to mark our passing. Holeb, too, was but an echo, now just a name and a few derelict shacks. Only the railroad and an occasional intrepid fisherman knew that it even existed. I knew Holeb once had had its place in the sun. It was a coaling station years ago in the time when freight trains east and west and four passenger trains a night paused there on their way across the north woods. It was also the point where customs and immigration officers laid over between trains. Holeb was one of those countless places in history that have an ephemeral grasp on existence, then whither and die when they are no longer useful. Ghost towns, a phenomenon of our industrialized world, where obsolescence is the specter of all America's Holebs.

Down past Boston Ranch and Elmer and Attean, whistle shrieking, we laid a trail of smoke roaring past lake and forest and Muskeg until civilization reappeared momentarily at Jackman Station where we stopped to get train orders and take water. When Bud climbed up into the cab with a fistful of orders he handed me a piece of paper.

"It's for you," he said. The message read:

To D. Plowden on train #518 at Jackman:
No. 517 will have diesel engine tomorrow, Wednesday.
—Wm. Laidlaw, Ch.Ds. Brownville Jct. 3/29/60

It was confirmed. Doug climbed back into the cab after filling the tender with water. Bud sat down and read the orders then handed them to Doug, who put them in a pocket of his coveralls. No one said anything for a long time. I just sat in silence listening to the sounds of the engine as it racketed along toward its rendezvous with history. I looked out the window and wondered if I would ever be as happy again. It was all going too fast, almost as if Bud wanted to finish the job as quickly as possible. Yet there was something in the way the whistle sounded, and that he blew it far more than necessary, which made me realize that perhaps the taciturn old Yankee had found a voice with which to express his feelings.

We made the usual stop at Onawa to take water and switch a few cars. As we started on our way again I realized that the train had been left behind and that the 5107 was heading over the viaduct by itself.

I looked at Doug.

"You want your picture, don't you?" he said smiling broadly. "Well, this is your last chance."

Then he explained that he and the rest of the crew had talked about my story of the picture in *Railroad Magazine* and had come up with a plan.

"We'll run you over, leave you on the other side, and we'll slow up just enough so you can catch the engine as we go by. We can't stop because we'll be on the grade by then. But you're an old railroader. You should have no trouble climbing aboard."

I admit I was aghast and not a little apprehensive.

We headed across the viaduct. When we reached the other side Bud stopped the engine and waited while I climbed down with my gear. Once on the ground I watched as the 5107 backed across the viaduct until it disappeared around the curve into Onawa. There I was all alone knee deep in snow in the middle of the wilds of Maine. My first thought was what would I do if the engine was going too fast when it came by? Would they really leave me out here? I seriously doubted it. Did I remember how to catch an engine? Yes. Catch the grab iron with my right hand, while thrusting my left foot into the corner of the bottom step of the ladder to the cab at exactly the same instant, then catch the other grab iron with my left hand in order to steady myself. I had done it many times before when I worked for the Great Northern. That had been four years ago and this time there was no chance to practice.

I remembered one incident only too well. Once I had caught a train when it was going too fast. The force of the impact pulled my right arm out of its socket. Goddamn that sonofabitch Burns, the brakeman, who hated the little "snot-faced" assistant to the trainmaster from Yale. "I can't. I can't catch it," I remember saying to him as we stood side by side in the snow waiting to catch the caboose of an accelerating freight train. "It's going too fast."

"Well you'd better 'cause there won't be another train along 'til Monday." It was Friday. I was miles from anything in the dead of winter on the windswept snowfields of South Dakota. I had no choice. I watched with my heart in my mouth as the caboose came into sight. I looked pleadingly at Burns, who ignored me as he caught the caboose's front steps. I remember only instinctively reaching for the curved grab iron by the rear steps and then the pain. Such pain I have never felt! And then seeing my right arm in front of my chest as I staggered onto the rear platform. I stayed out on the platform in a daze, tears streaming down my face, before I had the courage to shove my arm back in place. I was damned if I would let Burns see that I was hurt. I remember standing there for a long time before going inside and pouring a mug of coffee from the pot on the stove. For years afterward I had to sleep with a sling to prevent the shoulder from popping out and to this day I still feel the pain. And now it was with my right arm that I was going to have to catch the grab iron and lift myself up into the 5107.

There was no time to think about Burns and that disaster on the prairie. The sound of the engine whistling off from Onawa brought me back to the task at hand. Concentrate, Plowden! There is a picture to be made and this is your one and only chance to make it. Nothing else matters. Forget Burns. I heard the sound of the 5107's exhaust as it started up. I made sure that everything was ready: exposures, film in both the Rollei and the Leica—I always carry a spare camera. I knew the exact point on the bridge where the engine would be when I fired the shutter. Once again I chose to rely on my old Rolleiflex—the "toy," as Minor had always referred to it, derisively—to make the picture.

Suddenly the 5107 and the Scoot hove in view at the other end of the viaduct. I saw my photograph materializing before me in the form of a locomotive bearing down on me under a cloud of smoke and steam, whistling like a banshee from hell. I fired a test exposure, listening carefully to make sure the shutter was working properly in the cold, and advanced the film. Then I fired the shutter once again as insurance to make sure my picture would be near the center of the roll lest I kink the beginning of the roll in the process of developing it. Then I waited for what seemed an eternity until the 5107 reached the exact place on the viaduct I had chosen. I held my breath, fired the shutter. That was it. I threw the cameras across my back, turned, took a few steps toward the tracks. All at once the engine was upon me, suddenly transformed from a photograph into an immense, terrifying creature. I held my ground as the driving wheels and rods churned by just inches from my face. My eyes were riveted on the first step of the narrow ladder that led up to the cab. It drew closer. I gauged the distance; a vision of Burns, the pain as my arm tore out of its socket, flashed across my mind. No time for those thoughts now. I raised both my arms into position, as I had done so many times before. Okay Plowden. Now! My right arm instinctively reached for the right-hand grab iron at the same instant I thrust my left foot firmly into the corner of the bottom step as it drew abreast of me, then caught the left-hand grab iron with my good—my left —arm. Suddenly I felt the sensation of being lifted off the ground. I hoisted myself up the steps into the cab, very glad to be sitting safely on my seat box behind Doug once again.

"Did you get it?" I heard Bud say, as he pulled the throttle back all the way and the 5107 surged once more into full stride.

I had my souvenir.

Seventeen more miles. That was all that was left and it would be over. How does one savor the last moment? I sat there trying to make myself realize the importance of what was happening while it was happening. Nothing was different from the myriad other times I had ridden in the cab: the noise, the heat, the smell of coal and hot grease, all the gauges and, on the backhead, the handles on the throttle and brake valves worn smooth by years of

use. I was completely at home here. It was a place I took for granted as much as any room in my own house. I shut my eyes and listened.

I thought of my first trip across Maine on the CPR in August 1950. I was on Number 40, one of a brace of overnight trains between Montreal and St. John when this line was truly the High Iron to the Atlantic, which completed the Canadian Pacific's "trancontinentalness." I thought of Holeb where we took coal and where the customs and immigration officials came aboard. I remembered standing in the vestibule of my coach so as to hear our engine, Number 2396, fight its way up Johnville Hill out of Lennoxville. I was there, too, in the vestibule as we went into "the hole"—the passing track—at Ditchfield, so as not to miss Number 39 as it roared by, and at Attean as we waited for Number 41 with engine Number 2397. A coincidence, I thought, that two engines with consecutive numbers out of a class of 109 identical sisters should pass each other here at the same place at the same time. It was an absolutely clear moonlit night as I remember and the myriad lakes were all aglitter. The steam from the engine like a long cloud rolled across the sky, occasionally backlit by the moon. I sat up all night watching the steam and listening to the wail of the whistle. By first light I was waiting, starving, for the café parlor car to be put on at Mattawamkeag. I had one of those CPR breakfasts, which, as I remember, always featured blueberries and cream. I remember, too, watching dawn breaking over the wilderness and the sunlight catching the steam from the engine. How perfect: a steam engine up front, breakfast on the CPR, looking out the window for a moose.

I had to leave the train at Vanceboro, Maine, just a stone's throw from the border of New Brunswick. As I stood on the platform watching the 2396 being exchanged for Number 2307, another absolutely immaculately polished CPR Pacific, which would take Number 40 on to St. John, I realized at that moment the CPR was unquestionably my favorite railroad. The engine whistled off, leaving Vanceboro and me behind.

The magic was suddenly gone. The sun was high as I caught the Maine Central's local for Bangor and returned to the world of the diesel.

I wondered if those two sisters, the 2396 and the 2397, that had passed in the night had already been scrapped or were among those rows of doomed engines I had seen at Angus Shops a few weeks ago. Sadly none of that famous class of locomotives was to survive.

The sound of one long, long whistle aroused me from my reverie and announced to Brownville Junction that the Scoot was coming home. I heard the clatter of switches and looked out of the cab as the yard began to materialize. There was a little knot of people on the platform in front of the station. As we drew to a stop I saw a flashbulb pop and recognized Bill Laidlaw among the half dozen people gathered there. Bud and Doug came down from the cab and someone came up and said something to them. I gathered my gear and slid down the step onto the platform next to Bud and Doug. They stayed just long enough for me to take several photographs of them with the 5107. I thanked them for making the photograph on the viaduct possible and for letting me be in the cab with them on this occasion. We shook hands, said good-bye—and they were gone. I found Bill Laidlaw and thanked him for everything he had done for me. Suddenly the crowd dissipated. And that was all the ceremony there was.

I climbed back into the cab and rode back to the engine terminal with the hostler. Once there he went about servicing the 5107 as if it were going out on the Scoot again in the morning. He began to perform the rituals of service I had watched so many times before, but now they seemed almost macabre. First he backed the 5107 down to the coal dock and filled the tender with coal. Next he spotted the tender under the water plug and proceeded to fill it with water. Finally he moved the engine down to the ash pit where he meticulously lubricated and oiled the running gear. Then he took the fateful step. He dropped the fire, the ashes, and hot coals from the firebox. He backed the dying engine onto the turntable, turned it so that it faced the roundhouse, and with the steam still remaining in its boiler he put the 5107 in its stall.

I climbed up into the cab and sat there in complete solitude for several hours listening to the sounds I knew so well grow fainter and fainter. I kept glancing at the needle on the steam pressure gauge. Each time, the needle had dropped a little farther until it finally pointed to zero. I stayed for a few more minutes, unable to say a final farewell. When I was sure there was no more life left in the 5107 I climbed down from the cab and walked slowly past the driving wheels and connecting rods. As I came abreast of the main crankpin I stopped and put the back of my hand against it as I had seen many an engineer do. It was still warm. When I passed by the crosshead I reached out and ran my hand along the top guide of that

as well. It too was still warm and streaked with slowly congealing grease. When I reached the pilot beam at the very front of the engine I stopped again and looked up into its face, finally said one long, last farewell. I turned abruptly, then took a shower, packed my gear, and said good-bye to the hostler and to Brownville Junction.

I had done my "damned engines," poured my heart and soul into photographing them. And now they were gone.

As I drove away from Brownville Junction I turned on the radio in my car and heard the voice of an announcer say that on Sunday, March 27, 1960, the last steam-powered train in regular service on a main line in the United States had made its final run on the Grand Trunk Western Railway from Detroit to Durand, Michigan.

And what about the Scoot today, March 29, 1960? Obviously the news hadn't reached the outside world yet. Perhaps it never did. How fitting, I thought, to have been all alone with one of my beloved locomotives, far away from everything on this, the last day.

Whether the Scoot was ever pulled by a steam engine again after March 29 or whether the 5107 was ever fired up again is immaterial. What is important is that the continuity was broken that day in Brownville Junction. For me the age of the steam locomotive died there at dusk on March 29, 1960.

—David Plowden, March 1, 2010

CANADIAN PACIFIC RAILWAY, THE GLEN ENGINE TERMINAL, WESTMOUNT, QUEBEC, 1960.

LEFT AND ABOVE · CANADIAN PACIFIC RAILWAY, THE GLEN ENGINE TERMINAL, WESTMOUNT, QUEBEC, 1960.

CANADIAN PACIFIC RAILWAY, ENGINES BEING SERVICED, THE GLEN ENGINE TERMINAL, WESTMOUNT, QUEBEC, 1960.

QUEBEC CENTRAL RAILWAY, FIREMAN WATERING ENGINE, VALLÉE-JONCTION, QUEBEC, 1960.

CANADIAN PACIFIC RAILWAY, ENGINE TERMINAL MÉGANTIC, QUEBEC, MARCH 29, 1960.

CANADIAN PACIFIC RAILWAY, ST. LUC FREIGHT YARDS, MONTREAL, QUEBEC, 1960.

GREAT NORTHERN RAILWAY, "EXTRA 3387 EAST," NEAR WILLMAR, MINNESOTA, 1955.

GREAT NORTHERN RAILWAY, "EXTRA 3383 EAST," NEAR WILLMAR, MINNESOTA, 1955

GREAT NORTHERN RAILWAY, "EXTRA 3377 EAST," NEAR ATWATER, MINNESOTA, 1955.

GREAT NORTHERN RAILWAY, LOCOMOTIVE NUMBER 3383 ON FREIGHT TRAIN, LEAVING WILLMAR, MINNESOTA, 1955.

GREAT NORTHERN RAILWAY, "EXTRA 3383 EAST," KANDIYOHI, MINNESOTA, 1956.

42   CARTER, MONTANA, 1971.

AURELIA, IOWA, 1986.

UNION PACIFIC RAILROAD, RIGHT-OF-WAY, CHEYENNE WELLS, COLORADO, 1971.

COLORADO & SOUTHERN RAILWAY, GRENVILLE, NEW MEXICO, 1971.

GRAIN ELEVATORS, GOLDEN VALLEY, NORTH DAKOTA, 1971.

SOO LINE DEPOT, MARTIN, NORTH DAKOTA, 1968.

SOUTHERN PACIFIC / WESTERN PACIFIC RAILROAD, DEPOT, BEOWAWE, NEVADA, 1973.

ANTELOPE, MONTANA, 1971.

CATTLE CHUTE, ON NEVADA NORTHERN RAILWAY, CURRIE, NEVADA, 1973.

CHICAGO, MILWAUKEE, ST. PAUL & PACIFIC RAILROAD, RIGHT-OF-WAY, NEAR SCENIC, SOUTH DAKOTA, 1974.

GREAT NORTHERN RAILWAY, FREIGHT TRAIN, WEST OF HAVRE, MONTANA, 1968.

NORTHERN PACIFIC RAILWAY, FREIGHT TRAIN ASCENDING GRADE, WEST OF LIVINGSTON, MONTANA, 1954.

NORTHERN PACIFIC RAILWAY, FREIGHT TRAIN, NEAR ELLISTON, MONTANA, 1954.

NORTHERN PACIFIC RAILWAY, FREIGHT TRAIN, NEAR ELLISTON, MONTANA, 1954.

GREAT NORTHERN RAILWAY, "EXTRA 3377 EAST," NEAR ATWATER, MINNESOTA, 1956.

CENTRAL VERMONT RAILWAY, "EXTRA 464 NORTH" AND "EXTRA 472 SOUTH," AT AMHERST, MASSACHUSETTS, 1954.

STATION AGENT, BALTIMORE & OHIO RAILROAD, HARPERS FERRY, WEST VIRGINIA, 1961.

DELAWARE & HUDSON RAILROAD, "FA" TOWER, ONEONTA, NEW YORK, 1975.

MILWAUKEE ROAD, RIGHT-OF-WAY, WATERLOO, WISCONSIN, 1980.

TOLEDO, PEORIA & WESTERN RAILROAD AND ILLINOIS CENTRAL RAILROAD, DEPOT, EL PASO, ILLINOIS, 1968.

CANADIAN PACIFIC RAILWAY, FREIGHT TRAIN, HARVEY, NEW BRUNSWICK, 1959.

UNION STATION, NORTH CANAAN, CONNECTICUT, 1963.

QUEBEC CENTRAL RAILWAY, LEEDS, QUEBEC, 1960

QUEBEC CENTRAL RAILWAY, ENGINE TERMINAL, VALLÉE-JONCTION, QUEBEC, 1960.

SYDNEY & LOUISBURG RAILWAY, ENGINE TERMINAL, GLACE BAY, NOVA SCOTIA. 1959.

CHICAGO, MILWAUKEE, ST. PAUL & PACIFIC RAILROAD, ENGINE TERMINAL, BOZEMAN, MONTANA, 1954.

DENVER & RIO GRANDE WESTERN RAILROAD, CHAMA, NEW MEXICO, 1962.

SYDNEY & LOUISBURG RAILWAY, MIXED TRAIN AT LOUISBURG, NOVA SCOTIA, 1959.
BRAKEMAN ON PILOT BEAM OF OLD SYDNEY COLLIERIES LOCOMOTIVE, 1959.

CANADIAN PACIFIC RAILWAY, BRAKEMAN COUPLING LOCOMOTIVE NUMBER 5107 TO TRAIN NUMBER 518. MARCH 29, 1960.

DENVER & RIO GRANDE WESTERN RAILROAD, FREIGHT TRAIN ASCENDING GRADE TO CUMBRES PASS, COLORADO 1962.

DENVER & RIO GRANDE WESTERN RAILROAD, FREIGHT TRAIN ASCENDING 4 PERCENT GRADE TO CUMBRES PASS, COLORADO, 1962.

DENVER & RIO GRANDE WESTERN RAILROAD, FREIGHT TRAIN ASCENDING 4 PERCENT GRADE TO CUMBRES PASS, COLORADO, 1962.

UNION TRANSPORTATION COMPANY, NEAR NEW EGYPT, NEW JERSEY, 1959.

UNION TRANSPORTATION COMPANY, ENGINE TERMINAL, NEW EGYPT, NEW JERSEY, 1959.

CANADIAN PACIFIC RAILWAY, CODY, NEW BRUNSWICK, 1959.

VIRGINIA BLUE RIDGE RAILWAY, PINEY RIVER, VIRGINIA, 1961.

FIREMAN, LOCOMOTIVE NUMBER 9, VIRGINIA BLUE RIDGE RAILWAY. 1961.

BOB THOMBS, ENGINEER, CANADIAN PACIFIC RAILWAY, BROWNVILLE DIVISION, MAINE, 1959.
CANADIAN NATIONAL RAILWAYS, LOCOMOTIVE NUMBER 6218, WHITE RIVER JUNCTION, VERMONT, 1965.

CENTRAL VERMONT RAILWAY, ROUNDHOUSE, BRATTLEBORO, VERMONT, 1957.

DOUG BLUE, FIREMAN (L), AND BUD ROLF, ENGINEER (R) IN CAB OF CANADIAN PACIFIC RAILWAY LOCOMOTIVE NUMBER 5107, BROWNVILLE JUNCTION, MAINE, 1960.

FORMER LAKE SUPERIOR & ISHPEMING RAILROAD, LOCOMOTIVE NUMBER 23, MARQUETTE, MICHIGAN, 1975.

CANADIAN PACIFIC RAILWAY, MÉGANTIC, QUEBEC, MARCH 29, 1960.

CANADIAN PACIFIC RAILWAY, FREIGHT YARDS, MÉGANTIC, QUEBEC, MARCH 29, 1960.

CANADIAN PACIFIC RAILWAY, ENGINES BEING SERVICED, THE GLEN ENGINE TERMINAL, WESTMOUNT, QUEBEC, 1960.

CANADIAN PACIFIC RAILWAY, ENGINES BEING SERVICED, THE GLEN ENGINE TERMINAL, WESTMOUNT, QUEBEC, 1960.

CANADIAN PACIFIC RAILWAY, LOCOMOTIVE NUMBER 2461, VAUDREUIL, QUEBEC, 1960.

ENGINEER "OILING 'ROUND" LOCOMOTIVE, CANADIAN PACIFIC RAILWAY, THE GLEN ENGINE TERMINAL, WESTMOUNT, QUEBEC, 1960.

DRIVING WHEELS, READING COMPANY LOCOMOTIVE NUMBER 2124, SHAMOKIN, PENNSYLVANIA, 1962.

CENTRAL VERMONT RAILWAY, LOCOMOTIVE NUMBER 707, WHITE RIVER JUNCTION, VERMONT, 1957.

CLEANING FIRES, CENTRAL VERMONT RAILWAY, LOCOMOTIVE NUMBER 707, WHITE RIVER JUNCTION, VERMONT, 1957.

WASHING LOCOMOTIVE, CANADIAN PACIFIC RAILWAY, MCADAM, NEW BRUNSWICK, 1959.

SANDING, DENVER & RIO GRANDE WESTERN RAILROAD LOCOMOTIVE, CHAMA, NEW MEXICO, 1962.

HOSTLER CLEANING FIRES OF LOCOMOTIVE, WHITE RIVER JUNCTION, VERMONT, 1965.

COALING LOCOMOTIVE, CANADIAN PACIFIC RAILWAY, NUMBER 5137, BROWNVILLE JUNCTION, MAINE, 1959.

FIREMAN WATERING LOCOMOTIVE, UNION TRANSPORTATION COMPANY, NEW EGYPT, NEW JERSEY, 1959.

HOSTLER WASHING, VIRGINIA BLUE RIDGE RAILWAY LOCOMOTIVE, PINEY RIVER, VIRGINIA, 1960.
CANADIAN PACIFIC RAILWAY, PRESSURE WASHING LOCOMOTIVE, MCADAM, NEW BRUNSWICK, 1959.

DRIVING WHEELS, CANADIAN NATIONAL RAILWAYS, LOCOMOTIVE NUMBER 6218, WHITE RIVER JUNCTION, VERMONT, 1965.

CROSSHEAD, DETAIL, FORMER MILWAUKEE ROAD LOCOMOTIVE NUMBER 261, CHICAGO, ILLINOIS, 2004.

LOCOMOTIVE IN CANADIAN PACIFIC RAILWAY ROUNDHOUSE, ST. LUC ENGINE TERMINAL, MONTREAL, QUEBEC, 1960.

LOCOMOTIVE IN CANADIAN PACIFIC RAILWAY ST. LUC ROUNDHOUSE, MONTREAL, QUEBEC, 1960.

CROSSHEAD, DETAIL, CANADIAN NATIONAL RAILWAYS, LOCOMOTIVE NUMBER 6218, MONTPELIER JUNCTION, VERMONT, 1965.

MACHINIST IN ST. LUC ROUNDHOUSE, MONTREAL, QUEBEC, 1960.

CLEANING DRIVING WHEELS OF CANADIAN PACIFIC RAILWAY LOCOMOTIVE IN ROUNDHOUSE, THE GLEN ENGINE TERMINAL, WESTMOUNT, QUEBEC, 1960.

CANADIAN PACIFIC RAILWAY, LOCOMOTIVES IN ROUNDHOUSE, THE GLEN ENGINE TERMINAL, WESTMOUNT, QUEBEC, 1960.
CANADIAN PACIFIC RAILWAY, ST. LUC ROUNDHOUSE, MONTREAL, QUEBEC, 1960.

124   ABOVE AND RIGHT · CANADIAN PACIFIC RAILWAY, ST. LUC ROUNDHOUSE, MONTREAL, QUEBEC, 1960.

CANADIAN NATIONAL RAILWAYS LOCOMOTIVE IN ROUNDHOUSE, HAMILTON, ONTARIO, 1959.

HOSTLER WITH LOCOMOTIVE ON CANADIAN NATIONAL RAILWAYS TURNTABLE, HAMILTON, ONTARIO, 1959.

CANADIAN PACIFIC RAILWAY, ENGINE NUMBER 5107, ON TRAIN NUMBER 518, MARCH 29, 1960.

READING COMPANY, LOCOMOTIVES NUMBER 2124 AND NUMBER 2100, DOUBLE HEADING NEAR PORT CLINTON, PENNSYLVANIA, 1963.

CANADIAN PACIFIC RAILWAY, TRAIN NUMBER 518, THE SCOOT, CROSSING SHIP POND STREAM VIADUCT, ONAWA, MAINE, MARCH 29, 1960.

THE SCIOTOVILLE BRIDGE, CHESAPEAKE & OHIO RAILROAD, OHIO RIVER, SCIOTOVILLE, OHIO, 1968.

PITTSBURGH & LAKE ERIE RAILROAD BRIDGE, MONACA, PENNSYLVANIA, 1967.

CSX CORPORATION, COAL UNLOADING FACILITY, PRESQUE ISLE, OHIO, 1985.

CSX CORPORATION, HOPPER CAR IN COAL UNLOADING FACILITY, PRESQUE ISLE, OHIO, 1985.

LEFT AND ABOVE · INLAND STEEL COMPANY, EAST CHICAGO, INDIANA, 1979.

STEEL MILLS, BRADDOCK, PENNSYLVANIA, 1962.

SYDNEY & LOUISBURG RAILWAY, ENGINE TERMINAL AND DOSCO STEEL MILLS, SYDNEY, NOVA SCOTIA, 1959.

LTV STEEL COMPANY, INDIANA HARBOR WORKS, EAST CHICAGO, INDIANA, 1982.

U.S. STEEL COKE OVENS AND ELGIN, JOLIET & EASTERN RAILWAY YARDS, GARY, INDIANA, 1983.

NEW YORK CENTRAL AND PENNSYLVANIA RAILROAD YARDS, CHICAGO, ILLINOIS, 1966.

CENTRAL RAILROAD COMPANY OF NEW JERSEY, COMMUNIPAW TERMINAL, JERSEY CITY, NEW JERSEY, 1967.

CHESAPEAKE & OHIO RAILWAY YARDS, THURMOND, WEST VIRGINIA, 1974.

WATER PLUG, CHESAPEAKE & OHIO RAILROAD, THURMOND, WEST VIRGINIA, 1974.

COAL TIPPLE ON NORFOLK & WESTERN RAILWAY, WEST VIRGINIA, 1974.

NORFOLK & WESTERN RAILWAY YARDS, WELCH, WEST VIRGINIA, 1974.

CUMBERLAND, MARYLAND, AS SEEN FROM BALTIMORE & OHIO RAILROAD TRACKS, 1963.

RAILROAD STREET, PUTNAM, CONNECTICUT, 1975.

NORFOLK & WESTERN RAILWAY, RIGHT-OF-WAY, KEYSTONE, WEST VIRGINIA, 1974.

CENTRAL RAILROAD COMPANY OF NEW JERSEY, SKEW TRUSS, LEHIGHTON, PENNSYLVANIA, 1963.

STATION PLATFORM, DELAWARE & HUDSON RAILROAD, WHITEHALL, NEW YORK, 1965.

ERIE RAILROAD, DEPOT, DEPOSIT, NEW YORK, 1966.

CENTRAL RAILROAD COMPANY OF NEW JERSEY, DEPOT, WHITEHOUSE, NEW JERSEY, 1963.

CHESAPEAKE & OHIO RAILROAD, DEPOT, DELAWARE, OHIO, 1964.

LEHIGH VALLEY RAILROAD, DEPOT, SOUTH PLAINFIELD, NEW JERSEY, 1963.

LEHIGH VALLEY RAILROAD, DEPOT, ROCHESTER JUNCTION, NEW YORK, 1959.

BALTIMORE & OHIO RAILROAD, YARD OFFICE, EAST SALAMANCA, NEW YORK, 1975.

ERIE RAILROAD, DEPOT, THOMPSON, PENNSYLVANIA, 1966.

R. H. BIRKHEAD, AGENT, M-K-T RAILROAD, FREDERICK, OKLAHOMA, 1968.

CHICAGO & EASTERN ILLINOIS RAILROAD, DEPOT, PRINCETON, INDIANA, 1966.

CHICAGO & EASTERN ILLINOIS RAILROAD, DEPOT, PRINCETON, INDIANA, 1966.

PASSENGER DEPOT, KINGSTON, RHODE ISLAND, 1975.

WAITING ROOM, UNION STATION, CANAAN, CONNECTICUT, 1963.

ABOVE AND RIGHT · READING COMPANY, OUTER DEPOT, READING, PENNSYLVANIA, 1963.

WAITING ROOM, READING COMPANY, OUTER DEPOT, READING, PENNSYLVANIA, 1963.

CONCOURSE, READING COMPANY, OUTER DEPOT, READING, PENNSYLVANIA, 1963.

CENTRAL VERMONT RAILWAY, STATION, ST. ALBANS, VERMONT, 1963.

CENTRAL VERMONT RAILWAY, STATION, ST. ALBANS, VERMONT, 1963.

WESTBOUND PHOEBE SNOW, AT ERIE-LACKAWANNA RAILROAD STATION, SCRANTON, PENNSYLVANIA, 1964.

JOHN M. CAFFREY, CONDUCTOR, LEHIGH VALLEY RAILROAD, WILKES-BARRE, PENNSYLVANIA, 1959.

CANADIAN PACIFIC RAILWAY, WINDSOR STATION, MONTREAL, QUEBEC, 1960.

TRAINS DEPARTING, CANADIAN PACIFIC RAILWAY, WINDSOR STATION, MONTREAL, QUEBEC, 1960.

CANADIAN PACIFIC RAILWAY, THE GLEN ENGINE TERMINAL, WESTMOUNT, QUEBEC, 1960.

CANADIAN PACIFIC RAILWAY, LOCOMOTIVE DRIVING WHEEL, DETAIL, THE GLEN ENGINE TERMINAL, WESTMOUNT, QUEBEC, 1960.

CANADIAN PACIFIC RAILWAY, LOCOMOTIVE DEPARTING VANDREUIL, QUEBEC, 1960.

EXTENDED CAPTIONS

8 Canadian Pacific Railway locomotive Number 5107 at Lac-Mégantic, Quebec, on the morning of March 29, 1960, before departing for Brownville Junction, Maine, on train number 518, the Scoot. Number 5107 was a 2-8-2 type originally built by the Canadian Pacific's Angus Shops, Montreal, Quebec (CPR), as a class P-1a in 1912. It was rebuilt at the same Angus Shops, ca. 1926, reclassified as a P-1d and renumbered 5107. Mégantic, Quebec, March 29, 1960.

27 Engine crew at the Canadian Pacific Railway's Glen Engine Terminal, Westmount, Quebec. The Glen was the engine terminal that serviced all the CPR's passenger engines operating in and out of its Windsor Station, Montreal. It was the last and largest concentration of passenger steam locomotives in Canada and the United States. In March 1960, the time when all the photographs were made at the Glen, there were no more than

seven steam locomotives in service at any one time. All were used on commuter trains in and out of Windsor Station. Three were used to Riguad, three to Vaudreuil, and one to Farnham, Quebec.

28 Canadian Pacific Railway locomotive Number 2461, next to the last of the G-3h class 4-6-2s, on ready track in snowstorm at the Glen Engine Terminal. Photographed in March 1960.

29 Locomotive numbers 2820 and 1201 at the Glen Engine Terminal. Number 2820 was the first of the famous Royal Hudsons. Number 1201 and its sister Number 1200 were the first of the 101 celebrated G-5 4-6-2s and were the last locomotives built at the CPR's Angus Shops. Photographed in March 1960.

32 Canadian Pacific Railway locomotive Number 5107 and Number 3514, an M-4g-class 2-8-0 built by the Baldwin Locomotive Works (BLW) in 1907. Because the regular diesel switch engine was on snowplow duty, Number 3514 was the switch engine working the freight yards in Lac-Mégantic, Quebec, on March 29, 1960.

35-41 Great Northern Railway "Extra 3387 East" near Willmar, Minnesota. Locomotive Number 3387, an O-8 class 2-8-2 locomotive, was built in 1946. Photograph made in winter of 1955–56.

All of these photographs were made during 1955–56 while I was employed by the Great Northern Railway as an assistant to the trainmaster assigned to the Willmar Division in Minnesota. At the time all the Great Northern's steam operations were confined to lines east of Minot, North

Dakota. Happily for me the lion's share of the steam activity happened to be on the Willmar Division. All of the passenger trains and most of the freights on the main line between Breckenridge and Minneapolis, Minnesota, were diesel powered. However, in 1955–56 there were never enough diesels to go around, especially when extra power was needed for grain trains. When this occurred the Great Northern most often turned to its celebrated twenty-five O-8-class 2-8-2s to do the work. I knew them well, having ridden in the cabs on numerous occasions. During the winter of 1955-56 when these photographs were made there were five active O-8s on the Willmar Division: Numbers 3375, 3377, 3383, 3387, and 3396. By the end of 1956 most of the GN's steam had been stored. In July and August 1957 there was a brief revival of steam on the Willmar Division when six active locomotives made their last stand.

The O-8s were in a class by themselves. They were not only the heaviest 2-8-2s ever built, weighing 425,540 pounds, but they had the heaviest axle loading of any steam locomotive, 81,250 pounds. They were immense in other ways as well. The O-8s were among the most powerful 2-8-2s ever constructed. They had a tractive effort of 75,900 pounds. Their 69-inch driving wheels gave them more speed than the 63-inch drivers of the average 2-8-2 and their 28 x 32–inch cylinders coupled with 250 pounds of boiler pressure put them on a par with the 2-8-4. The Great Northern built the first three O-8s, Numbers 3397, 3398, and 3399, in 1932. The remaining twenty-two, Numbers 3375 to 3396, were rebuilt at the Great Northern's shops from O-7-class 2-8-2s from 1944 to 1946. All were equipped with roller bearings throughout. Although it has been stated that some O-8s burned coal, according to the Great Northern's own list of locomotive diagrams issued May 1956 all were oil burners. All were scrapped.

36 Great Northern Railway "Extra 3383 East" near Willmar, Minnesota. Locomotive Number 3383, an O-8-class 2-8-2, was built in 1944. Photograph made in winter of 1955–56.

37 Great Northern Railway "Extra 3377 East" near Atwater, Minnesota. Locomotive Number 3377, O-8 class 2-8-2, was built in 1945. Photograph made in winter of 1955–56.

39 Great Northern Railway locomotive Number 3383, an O-8 class 2-8-2, on freight train west of Willmar, Minnesota. Photograph made in winter of 1955–56.

41 Great Northern Railway "Extra 3383 East," Kandiyohi, Minnesota. Locomotive Number 3383, O-8 class 2-8-2, was built in 1944. Photograph made in winter of 1955–56.

47 Grain elevators beside Northern Pacific Railway tracks, Golden Valley, North Dakota. The grain elevators and the railway line have been abandoned since the photograph was made in 1971.

48 Soo Line Railroad depot, Martin, North Dakota. When last seen by me in 2005 there was nothing to indicate the depot ever existed. Photograph made in 1968.

53 The Chicago, Milwaukee, St. Paul & Pacific Railroad's right-of-way near Scenic, South Dakota. Construction on the line began at Marquette, Iowa, in 1880 with the intent to reach Rapid City, South Dakota. However, construction was halted at Chamberlain on the east bank of the Missouri River in 1881 because the west side of the river was part of the Sioux Reservation. After twenty years of negotiations the railroad was able to resume construction in 1906 and finally reach Rapid City in 1907. But things never went well for the railroad. By 1980 its several thousand miles of track in South Dakota were in such deplorable condition they were embargoed. In 1981 the state purchased much of the abandoned right-of-way including its Rapid City line. Part of this line was operated by the Dakota Southern Railway but only as far as Kadoka. The line west of there—on which this photograph was made in 1974—has not seen a train since 1980, and beginning in 1996 the rails, ties, and bridges were sold as scrap. On October 1, 2009, the Dakota Southern Railway was sold to new owners who plan to rehabilitate and operate the line to Murdo over the next three years.

57 Locomotive Number 5123, a class Z-7 4-6-6-4 or "Challenger" type built in 1941, on the point of Northern Pacific Railway freight train climbing the grade west of Livingston, Montana. Number 5010, one of the road's twelve Z-5 2-8-8-4s or "Yellowstone" type locomotives, is assisting it on the rear end. The Z-5s were monstrous machines. Number 5000, the first of the Yellowstones, was built in 1928 by Alco. It was followed by eleven more, delivered by Baldwin in 1930. At the time the Z-5 was the largest steam locomotive in the world. Noteworthy was the size of its firebox, which was designed to burn low-grade lignite called Rosebud coal found in mines along the NP's line in Montana. They were 9 feet wide and 22 feet and 2 inches long, so cavernous that Alco celebrated the 5000's debut by serving a dinner for twelve seated in the firebox.

Despite their size the Northern Pacific's Yellowstones were not good steamers and by the time I made this photograph in 1954 they had been relegated by the diesels to pusher service over Livingston Hill between Livingston and Bozeman, Montana. Because they did not live up to expectations the NP in 1936 sought a better locomotive and turned to the 4-6-6-4. Alco built all fifty of them in three lots, the last delivered in 1944.

58 Northern Pacific Railway locomotive Number 1840 at the head of a freight train near Elliston, Montana. It was one of 135 class W-3 2-8-2s built by Alco-Brooks between 1913 and 1920. According to Lloyd Stagner's article in the *National Railway Bulletin* (vol. 56, no. 4), in 1991, the last run of a Northern Pacific steam locomotive was made on January 17, 1958, on a Duluth, Minnesota–Superior, Wisconsin, transfer of one of these class W-3 2-8-2s, Number 1713.

61 Great Northern Railway "Extra 3377 East" near Atwater, Minnesota. Locomotive Number 3377, O-8 class 2-8-2, was built in 1945. Photograph made in spring of 1956.

63 Central Vermont Railway manifest freight train Number 491 running as Extra 464 North meets Extra 472 South at Amherst, Massachusetts, in April 1954. Extra 464 is actually double-headed. The second locomotive is obscured in the photograph. All three engines were class N-5-a 2-8-0s.

64 Baltimore & Ohio Railroad station agent at Harpers Ferry, West Virginia, about to "hoop up" orders to eastbound freight train. Photograph made in 1961.

65 Delaware & Hudson Railroad. "FA" tower in freight yards, Oneonta, New York. The D&H abandoned the Oneonta freight yards in 1980 when it was part of the Guilford Transportation Company and moved its operations to the former Delaware, Lackawanna & Western Railroad yards in East Binghamton, New York. Today there is nothing left of the D&H's vast complex in Oneonta. Photograph made in 1975.

67 Illinois Central Railroad and Toledo, Peoria & Western Railway joint freight station, El Paso, Illinois. It is currently vacant and not in use as a freight house. I believe it was added to the National Register of Historic Places in 1994. Photograph made in 1968.

68 Canadian Pacific Railway locomotive Number 5400 on freight train leaving Harvey, New Brunswick, in July 1959.

69 Canaan Union Depot, North Canaan, Connecticut. This board and batten Gothic revival gem was completed in 1872 at the junction of the Connecticut Western and the Housatonic Railroad (both later absorbed by the New York, New Haven & Hartford Railroad). G. H. Bundy, a local cabinetmaker and builder of coffins, is credited with its exceptional wooden carpentry. Passenger service ended April 30, 1971 Freight service has been provided by the Housatonic Railroad Company since 1983. The depot was added to the National Register of Historic Places on April 26, 1972. After being abandoned it was finally purchased and part of it turned into a restaurant. On the night of October 13, 2001, it was set afire by four teenage boys on a lark. Most of the east-west wing of the station was completely destroyed. However, the nonprofit Connecticut Railroad Historical Association purchased the entire property in 2003 and is in the process of rebuilding and restoring the station.

70 Canadian Pacific Railway locomotive Number 2541 on local freight arriving at Leeds, Quebec, on the Quebec Central Railway. Number 2541 was a class P-1e 4-6-2 built by the Montreal Locomotive Works in 1913 and was assigned to the QCR. Photograph made in March 1960.

71 Canadian Pacific Railway engine Number 1083, a D-10k-class 4-6-0 photographed at the Quebec Central Railway engine terminal at Vallée-Jonction, Quebec, in March 1960. The 1083 was built in 1912 by Alco Schenectady for service on the CPR's lines in Vermont. According to my notes this was its last day of its operation. The Quebec Central was completely dieselized a few days after I visited Vallée-Jonction in March 1960.

74 Chicago, Milwaukee, St. Paul & Pacific Railroad engine terminal Bozeman, Montana. Terminal, abandoned in 1980 when the Milwaukee's Pacific extension was abandoned west of Miles City, Montana. Photographed in 1954.

75 Denver & Rio Grande Western Railroad locomotive Number 494, a class K-37 2-8-2, at coal dock in Chama, New Mexico.

76 Sydney & Louisburg Railway locomotive Number 71 was one of the few locomotives purchased new by the S&L. It was a 2-8-2 built by the Montreal Locomotive Works in 1928 and was scrapped in 1961. Shown on mixed train at Louisburg, Nova Scotia, in August 1959.

77 Brakeman riding pilot beam of Old Sydney Collieries locomotive Number 18, a 0-6-0 type locomotive built by the Montreal Locomotive Works in 1911. Photographed in August 1959.

79 Brakeman coupling engine Number 5107 to train Number 518, the Scoot, on Canadian Pacific Railway's Moosehead subdivision, Maine, March 29, 1960.

80 Depicts the freight train I followed for two days climbing the 4 percent grade to Cumbres Pass, Colorado, elevation 10,015 feet. Locomotive Number 494, a class K-37 2-8-2, is on the point. Number 483, a class K-36 2-8-2, is pushing ahead of the caboose.

81 Denver & Rio Grande Western Railroad freight train working upgrade from Chama, New Mexico, to Cumbres, Colorado. It is the same train as depicted on pages **80** and **82**. Engine Number 483 is one of ten class K-36 engines built by the American Locomotive Company, Schenectady, New York, in 1925. They were the last engines built for the D&RGW's narrow-gauge lines.

82 Denver & Rio Grande Western Railroad locomotive Number 494 on freight train climbing the grade between Chama, New Mexico, and Cumbres, Colorado. The 494 is one of ten class K-37 engines that were rebuilt between 1928 and 1930 in the D&RGW's Burnham Shops in Denver from the boilers of standard-gauge C-41 class 2-8-0s, built by the Baldwin Locomotive Works in 1902. All four classes of the D&RGW's 2-8-2s were outside frame engines in which the driving wheels are squeezed between the narrow-gauge frames. The counterweights, crankpins, and driving rods are on the outside. Today twenty-two of the D&RGW 2-8-2s are still in existence. Seventeen of these twenty-two locomotives are owned by either the Durango & Silverton Narrow Gauge Railroad or the Cumbres & Toltec Scenic Railroad. They are either in use, stored serviceable, or unserviceable and used for parts. Another is owned by the Colorado Railroad Museum in Golden, Colorado; and a second is on static display

at Royal Gorge Park in Canon City, Colorado. One of the two surviving class K-27 locomotives, Number 464 is owned by the Huckleberry Railroad Museum in Michigan; and the other, Number 463, is owned by the Cumbres & Toltec Scenic Railroad.

The Durango & Silverton owns four K-36s, Numbers 480, 481, 482, and 486, and two K-37s, Numbers 493 and 498. The C&T owns six class K-36s, Numbers 483, 484, 485, 487, 488, and 489; it also owns four class K-37s, Numbers 492, 494, 495, and 497. The D&S owns three class K-28s, Numbers 473, 476, and 478.

83 Pennsylvania Railroad engine Number 5244 at Union Transportation Company's engine terminal, New Egypt, New Jersey. Photograph made June 1959.

84 Pennsylvania Railroad engine Number 5244, the last of the class B-6sb 0-6-0s, 238 of which were built by the Pennsylvania Railroad's Juniata Shop, Altoona, Pennsylvania, between 1916 and 1920. Shown on the Union Transportation Company's line near New Egypt, New Jersey, in June 1959. The UTC ceased operations in 1977 and its last tracks were torn up in 1984.

85 Canadian Pacific Railway locomotive Number 136, an A-2m-class 4-4-0 built in 1883 by the Rogers Locomotive and Machine Works, Paterson, New Jersey. The 136 and two other 4-4-0s, Number 29 and Number 144, were used in regular service on the CPR's Norton-Chipman Branch in New Brunswick until October 1959 because the bridge across Washademoak Lake was not strong enough to handle the weight of heavier engines. The branch was closed on March 31, 1962, because there was not enough traffic to warrant the strengthening of the old bridge. The 136, the 29, and the 144 were the oldest operating engines on the CPR at the time of their retirement. All have been preserved.

86 Virginia Blue Ridge Railway engine Number 9 at engine terminal, Piney River, Virginia. Number 9 was formerly a U.S. Army 0-6-0 built in November 1942 by the American Locomotive Company, Schenectady, New York, as USA No. 4023. It was one of eighty nearly identical class "060-155" locomotives (numbers 4000–4079), which were essentially USRA 0-6-0s, designed in World War I. Alco built the first forty-two and the last thirty-seven were built by the Lima Locomotive Company in 1942. Number 9 was sold to the Virginia Blue Ridge as war surplus by the War Assets Administration on August 8, 1958. The

VBR purchased two other 060-155s. USA No. 4039 was purchased on February 17, 1947, and No. 4038 on August 15, 1958. They became Numbers 5 and 8, respectively. All three were retired after the VBR was dieselized on August 1, 1966, and sold to various tourist railway lines.

The Virginia Blue Ridge Railway ran from Massies Mill, Virginia, to Tye River, where it connected with the Southern Railway. It was completed in 1915 to haul chestnut timber to local mills, but World War I and the chestnut blight put an end to this business. The VBR saw a resurgence of business when several chemical companies began to extract aplite and titanium dioxide from the area along the railway. All went well until Hurricane Camille severely damaged the railroad in 1969 and the Cyanamid company closed its plant in 1970. The Virginia Blue Ridge was finally abandoned in 1980. Part of the line is being turned into a trail. The photograph was made in 1961.

87 Fireman, Virginia Blue Ridge Railway engine Number 9 en route to Tye River, Virginia. The photograph was taken in 1961.

88 Bob Thombs, engineer, in cab of Canadian Pacific Railway locomotive Number 5137 on train number 517, the Scoot, between Brownville Junction, Maine, and Mégantic, Quebec. The Montreal Locomotive Works built number 5137 as a class P-1b 2-8-2 in 1913. It was rebuilt as a P-1e class, ca. 1926, at the Canadian Pacific's Angus Shops in Montreal. Photograph made July 23, 1959.

89 Canadian National Railways 4-8-4, class U-2g locomotive Number 6218 at White River Junction, Vermont, photographed in July 1965. The 6218 was built in September 1942 by the Montreal Locomotive Works. The CNR had a total of 160 4-8-4s in eleven classes, more than any other railroad. The Canadian Locomotive Company delivered the first, Number 6100, in 1927. It was given the name "Confederation" to commemorate the sixtieth anniversary of the Canadian Confederation. Thereafter all Canadian 4-8-4s—generally called the Northern type by most railroads—were known as Confederations. The last, Number 6264, was delivered in 1944.

It seems that the CNR kept steam locomotives on its roster for use on special excursions after the system was officially dieselized on April 25, 1960. Late in 1964, when the last of these engines, number 6167, came due for repairs, the 6218 was made ready to take over its duties at the CNR's Stratford, Ontario, shops. The 6218 made several excursions in Canada and, after being certified by the ICC, in the United States as well. One of these was the special excursion from St. Albans to White River Junction and return in July 1965 on which these photographs of the 6218 were made. The 6218 was finally retired on March 24, 1971, and moved to the Fort Erie Railway Museum in Fort Erie, Ontario, in October 1973, where it is on display. There is an interesting postscript to the CNR's steam excursions. Locomotive Number 6060, one of the twenty U1f-class 4-8-2s

built by the Montreal Locomotive Works in 1944 (they were the last steam engines built for the CNR), had been retired from active service in 1959 and subsequently placed on static display in 1962. Ten years later the CNR restored it to operating condition for excursion service out of Toronto. According to information provided by Frank Barry in 1976 the CNR announced it would run a special steam train that summer. Most interesting is the fact that the CN's summer timetables for 1976 and 1977 listed that steam special as Train No. 6060 scheduled between Toronto and Niagara Falls, Ontario. These trips were not excursions but bona fide scheduled passenger trains. The CNR gave the 6060 to the Province of Alberta on its centennial, in 1980. Today 6060 is currently owned and maintained by the Rocky Mountain Rail Society at Stettler, Alberta.

90 Central Vermont Railway Number 470, a class N-5a 2-8-0, rides the turntable at Brattleboro, Vermont. The sixteen N-5a-class engines, Numbers 460–475, were built by Alco Schenectady in 1923 and were the workhorses on the Central Vermont freight trains from White River Junction to New London, Connecticut. This photograph was made in late March 1957 shortly before the end of steam on the Central Vermont. On March 29 CNR 4-8-4 Number 6208 made the final run with the Montrealer from White River Junction to Montreal. April 4, 1957, was the last day of regular steam operation. On that day there were two final runs. One was by class U-1a 4-8-2 Number 602 on a freight train northbound from White River Junction. The other was by M-3a-class 2-8-0 Number 450 on train number 738, the "Palmer Turn," the local freight, from Palmer, Massachusetts, to Brattleboro, Vermont. The very last run was on May 20, 1957, when two CNR 4-8-4s took two sections of a special train from White River Junction to Montreal.

91 Engineer Bud Rolf (R) and fireman Doug Blue (L) on locomotive Number 5107. Brownville Junction, Maine, March 29, 1960.

93 One of the two last class-1 railroads to run steam locomotives was the Lake Superior & Ishpeming Railroad, a wholly owned subsidiary of the Cleveland-Cliffs Company, which served the iron ore mines of Michigan's Upper Peninsula. Before 1962, when it finally dieselized, the LS&I had eleven 2-8-0s in three classes in service. Numbers 18 to 23 were class SC-4, built by Alco Pittsburgh in 1910. Number 29 was built by Alco in 1906, and four more powerful engines, class SC-1, Numbers 32 to 35, were built by Baldwin in 1916. The LS&I abandoned its line to Big Bay, Michigan, in 1958 and then in 1962 sold it to the Marquette & Huron Mountain Railroad along with the eleven 2-8-0s. The M&HM had big plans to operate tourist trains and build a resort on Big Bay but they never materialized. The line defaulted and the LS&I repossessed the eleven locomotives and sold them to various tourist railways.

95 Canadian Pacific Railway locomotive Number 2663, a G-2u-7 class 4-6-2 built by the Canadian Pacific's Angus Shops. Photographed at Mégantic, Quebec, March 29, 1960, The 2663 made its final round trip from Sherbrooke to Mégantic on April 1, and returned to Sherbrooke a final time on April 2.

97 Canadian Pacific Railway yards at Lac-Mégantic, Quebec, on March 29, 1960. The three locomotives in service that morning were the 2663, the 5107, and the 3514.

98 Canadian Pacific Railway locomotive Numbers 2822 and 2825 were class H-1c 4-6-4s "Royal Hudsons." The Montreal Locomotive Works built a total of forty-five Royals in three classes. Numbers 2820–2849 were H-1c, built in 1937; Numbers 2850–2859 were class H-1d, built in 1938; and the last, 2860–2864, class H-1e, built in 1940, were oil burners. All sixty-five were examples of Henry Bowen's influence on the design of the CPR's locomotives. Among the most successful streamlined locomotives were Henry Blaine Bowen's creations for the Canadian Pacific that eventually I would come to know so well. Bowen, who was born in England, was the CPR's Chief of Motive Power and Rolling Stock from 1928 until 1949. He was an avowed "steam fanatic," who said in 1935, "The diesel engine of today, wonderful as it is, is doubtful as a lasting standard and it seems a reasonable prediction that it will be considered obsolete in a short period of years." Sadly he was wrong. However, during his tenure the CPR continued to build steam locomotives until its last one was delivered in 1949 the year he retired. During his forty-one years with CPR he was responsible for the design of the line's immense stable of locomotives including those which might best be called "semi-streamlined" locomotives. Unlike so many other attempts at modernization Bowen's creations did not impinge on the essence of the machine itself. His designs were not universally appreciated especially among U.S. rail aficionados who by and large felt they were too European for American sensibilities. At first even I found them somewhat of an acquired taste. However, I grew to love them fiercely, in 1959 and 1960, when I went to photograph them in their final hours. Photograph made in March 1960 at the Glen Engine Terminal.

99 Canadian Pacific Railway locomotive Number 2822, an H-1c-class 4-6-4 type locomotive being serviced at Glen Engine Terminal, Westmount, Quebec.

101 Canadian Pacific Railway locomotive Number 2461, photographed at Vaudreuil, Quebec, one morning in March 1960 when the temperature was fifteen below zero.

102 Engineer oiling 'round Canadian Pacific Railway locomotive 2461, a G-3h-class 4-6-2, prior to departure from the Glen Engine Terminal, Westmount, Quebec, in March 1960.

103 Driving wheel detail. Reading Company T-1-class 4-8-4 locomotive Number 2124. Photograph was made in 1963 on an "Iron Horse Ramble" in Shamokin, Pennsylvania.

The Reading's thirty T-1-class engines were erected in the railroad's own shops between 1945 and 1947 using the boilers from I-1a-class 2-8-0s that had been built from 1923 to 1925. The T-1s were notable for their extremely wide fireboxes—94.5 square feet—which extended beyond the locomotive's frame. This type of firebox was patented by James Wooten, superintendent of motive power for the Philadelphia & Reading, later the Reading, in 1877. The Wooten firebox was especially designed to burn waste anthracite coal known as culm, a by-product of the process of breaking and washing the coal. It was slow burning and required a very large grate area. The Wooten firebox was widely used by other "anthracite roads" such as the Delaware & Hudson, the Delaware, Lackawanna & Western, the Lehigh Valley, the Central Railroad Company of New Jersey, the Lehigh & New England, and the New York, Ontario & Western. The Reading was officially dieselized in 1956, however, in 1959, the railroad announced that an "Iron Horse Ramble" would be operated by one of its T-1-class 4-8-4s, Number 2124, on October 25. Subsequent "rambles" proved to be such a success that three more T-1s were withdrawn from storage, Numbers 2100, 2101, and 2102. The Reading continued to operate the rambles for nearly four more years until the cost of maintaining the engines was too great. In all there were a total of fifty. The last one ran on October 17, 1964. The 2124 was retired in October 1961 and was sold to Steamtown in Scranton, Pennsylvania, in July 1963. The 2101 was the standby locomotive for the Rambles but was never used on them, though it had the most illustrious career of all. It was sold as scrap in 1965 and rescued by Ross Rowland in 1974 who restored it. It became one of the three locomotives that pulled the American Freedom Train in 1975–76. From 1977 to 1979 it was the engine on the Chessie Special. Sadly it was severely damaged in a roundhouse fire in 1979. It was cosmetically restored and now is on static display at the Baltimore & Ohio Museum in Baltimore, Maryland. The 2102 eventually was sold and resold to numerous tour operators and was best known on the Blue Mountain & Reading in Hamburg, Pennsylvania, where it was used from 1985 until the early 1990s. In 1998 it was moved to the Reading, Blue Mountain & Northern Railroad's new shops at Port Clinton, Pennsylvania, where the RBN&N plans to restore it and run it a soon as possible. The 2100 had a rather peripatetic life after being sold to the same scrap yard in Baltimore as its two sisters (2101 and 2102). It was rescued in 1975 and for the next thirty years it was sold, resold,

rebuilt, and stored many times in many places, all too numerous to mention. It was sold again in 2005 to the Golden Pacific Railroad in Tacoma, Washington.

105 Locomotive Number 707 on turntable at White River Junction, Vermont. The 707 was the sole survivor of the ten class T-3a 2-10-4s, Texas-type locomotives built for the Central Vermont Railway by Alco Schenectady in 1928. The 700s were the largest locomotives in New England and were used primarily by the Central Vermont on its manifest freights on the line over the Green Mountains between St. Albans and White River Junction, Vermont. Occasionally they were used on the Connecticut River line as far south as Brattleboro, where I knew them so well. Weighing 419,000 pounds they were the lightest 2-10-4s ever built; nonetheless they were too heavy for the bridges and tracks beyond Brattleboro. This photograph was made in late March 1957 on what I was told was the 707's last southbound trip before being retired. I know for a fact the 707 was scrapped in November 1959.

107 Canadian Pacific Railway F-1a "Jubilee"-class 4-4-4 locomotive built by the Canadian Locomotive Company being washed in engine terminal, McAdam, New Brunswick, in July 1959.

108 Denver & Rio Grande Western Railroad locomotive Number 494 having its sand dome filled at Chama, New Mexico, in July 1962.

111 Fireman watering tender of Pennsylvania Railroad class B-6sb 0-6-0 engine Number 5244, leased to Union Transportation Company, New Egypt, New Jersey. Number 5244 was the last PRR engine in revenue service and made its last run on July 14, 1959. It was returned to Pennsylvania at Lewistown, New Jersey. Then it was run to the PRR's 46th Street engine house in Philadelphia, where the fires were finally dropped. Photograph made June 1959.

112 Hostler washing Virginia Blue Ridge Railway locomotive Number 8 at Piney River, Virginia. The photograph was made in 1961.

113 Canadian Pacific Railway locomotive Number 5400, a P-2f 2-8-2 built in 1928 by the Montreal Locomotive Works (MLW), being washed at the engine terminal in McAdam, New Brunswick, July 1959. At the time of my first trip to McAdam in the summer of 1959 it was the focal point of operations for the east end of the CPR's Atlantic Region. It was home base for a variety of steam locomotives: 2-8-2s, 4-6-2s, 4-6-0s, several 0-8-0 switchers, and even a lone class F-1a 4-4-4 assigned to local freight duty. When I revisited McAdam in late March 1960 it was virtually dead. The 5400 was in the scrap line with many other locomotives I had photographed. It was all but dead until the morning of April 7, 1960, when class D-10 4-6-0 Number 1077, built by the American Locomotive Company in Schenectady, New York (Alco Schenectady), in 1912, was fired up to run between McAdam and St. Stephen. According to Frank Barry, this was the last run of a steam locomotive in New Brunswick.

115 Locomotive Number 261 was formerly owned by the Milwaukee Road. It was one of ten class S-3 4-8-4s built in 1944 by the American Locomotive Company. When it was retired in August 1954 it was donated by the railroad to the National Railway Museum in Green Bay, Wisconsin, the present owners. The 261 was leased by an organization called the Friends of the 261 who rebuilt the locomotive at a former Burlington Northern shop in Minneapolis Junction in Minneapolis, Minnesota, 1993. The Friends ran the 261 on numerous excursions until September 2008 when its boiler ran out of its fifteen-year 1472 certification. Before it is able to be recertified and run again the 261 will have to be disassembled and inspected. This should not be a problem except that the Friends' fifteen-year lease on the engine will expire in two years and they want an extension before they expend some $500,000 in repairs on a locomotive they can keep for only two more years. The organization righty feels the museum's terms for a new lease are unreasonable. The museum held firm and the Friends will return the 261 to the museum. However, as of March 2010 it is rumored that the 261 will be sold to a private party. Whether it will every run again has not been determined. If it does not it will be a great loss as the 261 is one the few large serviceable steam locomotives in existence.

117 Canadian Pacific Railway locomotive 2816 was one of ten H-1b-class 4-6-4s built by MLW in 1930. When I photographed, in March 1960, it was stored dead in the roundhouse at the St. Luc engine terminal, Montreal, Quebec. Shortly before I left it was returned to service and was used in the Montreal commuter engine pool. It made its final run on May 26, 1960, from Rigaud to Montreal. The 2816 was to have a second life. Enter F. Nelson Blount, the millionaire founder of the Blount Seafood Corporation, who used his fortune to buy and preserve steam locomotives. In 1963 the 2816 was purchased by Blount's Monadnock, Steamtown & Northern Amusements Corp. The following year the company became Steamtown and the collection was moved to a site recently abandoned by the Rutland railroad near Bellows Falls, Vermont. After Blount's untimely death in his small plane on August 31, 1967, Steamtown began to fall on hard times. Seventeen years later in 1984 the Steamtown Foundation moved the collection, including the 2816, to Scranton, Pennsylvania. The National Park Service took over in 1986 and established the Steamtown National Historic Site in 1995. In 1998 the Canadian Pacific purchased the 2816 from the National Park Service and moved it to BC Rail's steam shops at North Vancouver, British Columbia. It reemerged in 2001 after a two-year, $2 million restoration as the "Empress." It was moved to Calgary, Alberta, and began its second career as a roving "ambassador" for the Canadian Pacific. However, at the end of 2008 the CPR's steam program was put on hold due to the poor economy and the 2816 was placed in storage in Calgary. At this date its fate has yet to be determined.

118 Canadian Pacific Railway locomotive Number 5145 was originally built by the Montreal Locomotive Works (MLW) in 1913 as a P-1b-class 2-8-2. It was rebuilt as a P-1e class ca. 1926 at the Canadian Pacific's Angus Shops in Montreal. It is shown in the roundhouse at St. Luc engine terminal, Montreal, Quebec. St. Luc was the CPR's main freight yard and engine terminal in the Montreal area and was one of if not *the* largest concentration of steam power in Canada and the United States at the time I made the photograph in March 1960.

120 Machinist checking air pumps of Canadian Pacific locomotive in the roundhouse at the Glen Engine Terminal, Westmount, Quebec, March 1960.

121 The Canadian Pacific was known for keeping its equipment in tip-top condition. Workers continued to wash down their locomotives after every assignment until the very end. A G-3g- or G-3h-class 4-6-2 being washed in the Glen roundhouse, March 1960.

122 Canadian Pacific Railway locomotive Number 2408, a G-3g-class 4-6-2 built by the Canadian Locomotive Company (CLC) in 1942. Photographed in the roundhouse at the Glen Engine Terminal, Westmount, Quebec.

123 Canadian Pacific Railway locomotive Number 1262 backing out of roundhouse in St. Luc engine terminal, Montreal, Quebec. Number 1262 was a class G-5c 4-6-2 built by the Canadian Locomotive Company in 1946. The 102 G-5 class locomotives delivered to the CPR between 1944 and 1948 were built to replace much older engines of the same type. Number 1301, the last of its class, delivered in 1948, was the very last 4-6-2 type locomotive built in North America. Several have found their way to tourist lines in the United States, where they are still in use.

124 Repairs to smoke box of Canadian Pacific Railway G-5c locomotive Number 1263 in roundhouse at St. Luc engine terminal, Montreal, Quebec. Photograph made in March 1960.

126 Canadian National Railways locomotive Number 8403 backing out of roundhouse, Hamilton, Ontario. Number 8403 was a class P-5h 0-8-0 type built in September 1930 by the Canadian National Railways' own Transcona shops in Winnipeg, Manitoba. It was scrapped in May 1961. Photograph made May 10, 1959, during last week of steam operation in Hamilton.

127 In May 1959 Hamilton, Ontario, was the last place on the vast CNR system east of Fort William, Ontario, where steam engines were still being used. The last regularly steam-powered train on the main line between Montreal and Toronto ran on April 17, 1959, with 4-8-4 Number 6214, just a few weeks before my visit to Hamilton. A year later steam was confined to a few lines in the Winnipeg, Manitoba, area. By most accounts the very last run of a Canadian National steam locomotive on a regularly scheduled train was made from the Pas Manitoba to Winnipeg on April 25, 1960. The engine was a class U-1d 4-8-2, Number 6043, built by the Canadian Locomotive Company in 1929.

129 Canadian Pacific Railway locomotive Number 5107, a class P-1d 2-8-2 on the Scoot, March 29, 1960.

131 Reading Company locomotive Numbers 2124 and 2100 double-heading the first "Iron Horse Ramble," approaching Port Clinton, Pennsylvania, October 25, 1959.

132 Canadian Pacific Railway's train Number 518, the Scoot, with locomotive Number 5107 crossing Ship Pond Creek viaduct east of Onawa, Maine, March 29, 1960.

133 The Sciotoville Bridge. Completed for the Chesapeake & Ohio Railway in 1917. Two 775-foot continuous through truss spans. This bridge was designed by Gustav Lindenthal, one of the most renowned bridge engineers of his day. Lindenthal was also the chief engineer

of the Hell Gate Bridge over the East River in New York City. The Sciotoville Bridge is, in the words of architecture historian Carl Condit, "the ultimate expression of mass and power among American truss bridges." Upon its completion the bridge was by far the largest truss of its kind ever built and in many ways it was the ultimate in railroad bridge design. It was gigantic in every respect and was designed to carry 78,800 pounds per linear foot, the highest combined live and dead loads of any bridge. Photographed in 1968.

135 Pittsburgh & Lake Erie Railroad bridge, Ohio River, Monaca, Pennsylvania. Through pin–connected cantilever and simple truss. Main span: 769 feet. Overall length: 1,787 feet. Albert Lucius, consulting engineer and designer. McClintic-Marshall Construction Company, contractor. Completed 1910. Photographed 1967.

136 CSX Corporation, former Chesapeake & Ohio Railway coal-loading facilities, Port of Toledo, Ohio. Photograph made in 1985.

137 Same location as in image on page **136**. Interior of car-dumping machinery.

138 Inland Steel Company High Line, beside "Blast Furnace Row," Indiana Harbor Works, East Chicago, Indiana. Photograph made in 1979.

139 Mould yard, Inland Steel Company, East Chicago, Indiana. Inland Steel's sole mill was its Indiana Harbor Works at East Chicago. In its heyday in 1969 it employed twenty-five thousand workers and was one of the largest steel mills in North America. Inland Steel was sold in 1998 and today is part of ArcelorMittal. Photograph made in 1979.

140 Steel mills, Braddock, Pennsylvania, as seen from Pittsburgh & Lake Erie Railroad right-of-way. Photograph made in 1962.

141 Sydney & Louisburg Railway engine terminal, Sydney, Nova Scotia. At the time I made this photograph in August 1959 the S&L was owned by the Dominion Steel & Coal Company. It was primarily a coal hauler and its proximity to Cape Breton's coal mines kept the S&L in steam until it was finally dieselized in 1961. Most of the locomotives on the S&L's roster were bought secondhand from U.S. railroads, which made it a working museum of engines belonging to a variety of railroads that had long ago dieselized. Among these were examples from the Chicago & Eastern Illinois, the New York Central, the Pittsburgh & Lake Erie, the Pere Marquette, the Chicago & Illinois Midland, the Michigan Central, and the Cambria & Indiana. Number 103, shown in this photograph, was built by the Baldwin Locomotive Company in 1928. It was one of three 2-8-2 types purchased from the Detroit & Toledo Shore Line in 1952. It was scrapped in 1960. Number 73 was also a 2-8-2 that had a long pedigree. It was built by Baldwin in 1912 as New Orleans, Mobile & Chicago Number 101. Next it was Gulf, Mobile & Northern's 101 and then Tennessee, Alabama & Georgia's Number 202. Its final incarnation was as S&L's Number 73. It was

scrapped in the spring of 1961. According to the most reliable source the S&L's last operating steam engines were Numbers 88 and 90. Number 88 was formerly Pittsburgh & Lake Erie Railroad Number 8042, a class U-3k 0-8-0 built by the Lima Locomotive Works, Lima, Ohio, in 1937. It was purchased by the S&L in 1955 and was reportedly scrapped shortly after its fires were dropped in November 1961. Number 90 was also a P&LE U-3k 0-8-0 built by Lima in 1937. It came to the S&L in February 1955 and was also retired in 1961 and scrapped in the same month and year as Number 88.

The steel mill in the photograph was originally Dominion Steel & Iron, which became Dominion Steel & Coal in 1930. The Hawker-Siddley Group purchased the mill in 1957. Ten years later it became SYSCO when the government of Nova Scotia assumed control. The mill was closed in 2001 and demolition was complete in 2005. The S&L became the Devco Railway when the Coal Division of the Cape Breton Development Corporation (DEVCO) took over the operations of the S&L on March 30, 1968. Photograph made in August 1959.

142 LTV Steel, Indiana Harbor Works, East Chicago, Indiana. Photograph made in 1983.

143 Elgin, Joliet & Eastern Railroad yards and United States Steel Corporation, Gary, Indiana, Works coke plant. Photograph made in 1983.

145 The Pennsylvania and the New York Central Railroad freight yards and right-of-way looking south toward Calumet River bridges, Chicago, Illinois. Photograph made in 1966, two years before the PRR and the NYC were merged into Penn-Central in 1968.

147 Central Railroad Company of New Jersey Communipaw Terminal throat tracks, Jersey City, New Jersey. This was the terminus for the CNJ's passenger trains until April 30, 1967, when it was abandoned after the Aldene Plan went into effect, which allowed all passenger trains using the terminal to gain access to New York's Penn Station. Photograph made in 1966.

architect Bradford Gilbert, who also designed the famous Tower Building in New York City. Gilbert designed many railroad stations in his career, notably Chicago's Central Station and the Intercolonial Railway of Canada's station at Halifax, Nova Scotia. The White House depot is one of the few surviving examples of his work and was listed on the National Register of Historic Places when it was restored as a library in 1981.

150 Coal tipple beside Norfolk & Western Railway right-of-way, McDowell County, West Virginia. Photograph made in 1974.

157 Central Railroad company of New Jersey over Lehigh Valley Railroad, Lehighton, Pennsylvania. One skew through Pratt truss span. Completed 1910. Abandoned 1972 when CRR of NJ line was abandoned. Photographed 1963.

148,149 Thurmond, West Virginia, was once the quintessential railroad town. Its "main street" was the main line of the Chesapeake & Ohio Railway, whose yard, coaling station, and engine terminal were wedged into what little flat land there was between the surrounding hills and the New River. Two banks, two hotels, two dry goods stores, and several other establishments faced the tracks. Until 1921 if you wanted to get to Thurmond you took the train. Today the only access by road is by way of a single lane cantilevered on the side of a railroad bridge over the river. During its heyday in the early 1900s Thurmond was one of the most important coal shipping stations on the C&O, producing more revenue from the surrounding mines than most other points on the system. Like so many other towns that depended on coal for their existence its place in the sun was not to last. Hard hit by the depression of the 1930s it began to wither. By the 1950s it had become virtually a ghost town—except for the C&O. When the C&O dieselized late in 1956 Thurmond was no longer needed by the railroad as a coaling and water station. For almost thirty years Thurmond languished, until 1984, when the entire town was designated a historic district. The district includes the railroad station, built in 1909, which has been restored and is a Park Service visitor center. Photographs made in 1974.

151 Norfolk & Western Railway freight yards, Welch, West Virginia. Photograph made in 1974.

155 Norfolk & Western Railway right-of-way through Keystone, West Virginia. Photograph made in 1974.

159 Erie Railroad passenger depot, Deposit, New York. Passenger service ended November 28, 1966. The building was razed shortly after Conrail took over the Erie-Lackawanna Railroad in 1976. Photograph made in 1966.

161 Former Central Railroad Company of New Jersey depot, White House, New Jersey. It closely resembles H.H. Richardson's style, and was built in 1892 and designed by the noted

163 Lehigh Valley Railroad depot, South Plainfield, New Jersey. Lehigh Valley discontinued all passenger service on February 3, 1961. Photograph made in 1963.

164 Lehigh Valley Railroad Station, Rochester Junction, New York. Destroyed by fire 1973. After Conrail absorbed the Lehigh Valley in 1976 the portion of its main line through Rochester Junction was abandoned. Photograph made in 1959.

165 Yard office, Baltimore & Ohio Railroad, East Salamanca, New York. East Salamanca was once the location of an important locomotive back shop, roundhouse, and freight yard on the Buffalo, Rochester & Pittsburgh Railway. The BR&P was absorbed by the B&O in 1932. The B&O was itself absorbed by the Chesapeake & Ohio in 1962 and became the Chessie System, which in turn merged with several other railroads. The final result was the CSX System, formed in 1980. The CSX divested itself of the former BR&P lines in 1988, which became the Buffalo & Pittsburgh Railroad, part of the Genesee & Wyoming's family of railroads. Today much of the old BR&P has been abandoned and all vestiges of East Salamanca's importance as a major railroad town have vanished. Only the old passenger station survives today as a museum. Photograph made in 1975.

166 The depot at Thompson, Pennsylvania, was one of seven virtually identical structures erected by the Erie Railroad in 1870. Almost immediately afterward the Delaware & Hudson Railroad leased the line from the Erie and eventually purchased it in 1955. In 1980 the D&H moved its trains through Binghamton, New York, and the line through Thompson was torn up in 1984. Today the depot is used as an ice cream parlor. Photograph made in 1966.

167 Ray H. Birkhead, agent Missouri-Kansas-Texas Railroad, Frederick, Oklahoma. Photograph made in July 1968 on the day of his retirement after sixty years with the railroad. I was the only person present in the station that afternoon and I asked him if he would pose for his portrait in order to commemorate the occasion. He gave his address and several months later I sent him a print. It was returned with the stamp: "Addressee Unknown." All I know is that he and his wife moved to Tallahassee, Florida, in 1969, where he died on April 4, 1971, without ever having seen the portrait I made for him.

168, 169 Chicago & Eastern Illinois railroad depot, Princeton, Indiana. Originally built for the Evansville & Terre Haute Railroad in 1875. Train service ended in 1968. Slated for demolition in 1987, the depot was saved and turned into a library by a local group known as the Princeton Railroad Station, Inc., which has a ninety-nine-year lease on the property.

170 The Kingston Railroad Station, West Kingston, Rhode Island. Erected in 1875 for the New York, Providence & Boston Railroad (later absorbed by the New York, New Haven & Hartford Railroad) it has been in continual use as a railroad passenger station ever since. However, throughout its long life it has undergone many transformations. After a long period of neglect during the Penn-Central era of the 1970s it was taken under the wing of local citizens who sought to repair and restore it. It was placed on the National Register of Historic Places on April 26, 1978. On December 12, 1988, the interior was badly damaged in a fire. However, the Friends of the Kingston Railroad Station obtained a grant from the National Trust for Historic Preservation to restore the damage. After 1996 when Amtrak began to upgrade the Northeast Corridor it was moved back from the tracks in order to accommodate a high-level platform. Photograph made in 1975.

171 Waiting room, Union Station, Canaan, Connecticut, 1963. See extended caption for page **69**.

172-175 Outer Depot, Reading, Pennsylvania, very ornate structure built in the triangular space between three lines of the Reading Company's tracks. It was built in 1874. After being abandoned following the cessation of train service ca. 1964 it was totally destroyed by fire on February 21, 1978. Photographs made in 1963.

177, 178 Train shed, Central Vermont Railway Station, St. Albans, Vermont. Unique four-track, brick train shed with its roof supported by a series of 88-foot curved Howe trusses. Built ca. 1866–67 by the contracting firm Harris and Hawkins of Springfield, Massachusetts. The structure was razed in September 1963.

179 Railroad station, Scranton, Pennsylvania, showing westbound Phoebe Snow under the train shed. The station was built in 1907–8 for the Delaware, Lackawanna & Western Railroad. The architect for the station proper was Kenneth Murchison, who designed a five-story neoclassical revival–style edifice fronted by six massive Doric columns. Lincoln Bush, the railroad's chief engineer, was responsible for the train shed. It was a unique structure he himself invented, in which the entire platform is covered except for a slot over the tracks that allows the smoke and steam from the locomotive to be discharged—a vast improvement over the immense, vaulted train sheds that covered as many as twenty-five or thirty tracks in a single span.

The streamliner Phoebe Snow was born on November 15, 1949, as a replacement for the Lackawanna Limited between Hoboken, New Jersey, and Buffalo, New York. The Phoebe was just one example of the postwar streamliners launched by America's railroads in an effort to attract passengers, which resulted in a whole fleet of beautiful trains. The effort proved to be futile, however, as Americans flocked to the automobile and airplanes in droves. By the 1960s trains like the Phoebe Snow and stations like the one at Scranton had become white elephants. On October 17, 1960, old rivals the Erie and the Lackawanna merged to form the Erie-Lackawanna. The first order of business for the new company was to eliminate duplicated services. On April 30, 1961, the Phoebe Snow became the Erie-Lackawanna Limited en route to Chicago. In October 1963 the name Phoebe was resurrected. By then, however, the age of the passenger train was drawing to a close. Most long-distance passenger trains relied more on mail and express revenue than on passenger fares. In 1966 the U.S. postal department notified the E-L that is was going to end its mail contract. The railroad, wanting to be rid of its money-losing passenger trains,

lost not a moment. It filed notice with the ICC to discontinue the Phoebe Snow, which made its last run on November 28, 1966. All passenger service was discontinued in January 1970 and the station was closed. The E-L eventually became part of Conrail, which finally sold the station in 1983. Today the Scranton station is the Scranton Radisson Hotel. Photograph made in 1964.

181 John M. Caffrey, conductor, Lehigh Valley Railroad train Number 26, the Asa Packer. Wilkes-Barre, Pennsylvania. Photograph made in 1959.

182 Canadian Pacific Railway conductor handing orders to engineer in cab of locomotive Number 2822 on commuter train, Windsor Station, Montreal, Quebec, March 1960.

185 Canadian Pacific Railway locomotive Number 2412, a G-3g-class 4-6-2 built by the Canadian Locomotive Company in 1942, photographed at the Glen Engine Terminal, Westmount, Quebec. The 2412 was another example of Bowen's influence. One hundred and two of these beautifully designed engines, like the 2412, Numbers 2351–2462, were delivered by CLC between 1938 and 1944. Sadly none survive.

187 Canadian Pacific Railway locomotive Number 2408, a G-3g-class 4-6-2 built in 1944 on a commuter train at Vaudreuil, Quebec, in March 1960. The CPR used steam locomotives in Montreal commuter service until June 1960. They were the last regularly scheduled standard-gauge-steam-powered passenger trains in Canada and the United States.